Do You, Without Them

Do You, Without Them

CALVIN RICHARDSON

Mechanicsburg, PA USA

Published by Sunbury Press, Inc.
Mechanicsburg, Pennsylvania

www.sunburypress.com

For information about special discounts for bulk purchases, please contact Sunbury Press Orders Dept. at (855) 338-8359 or orders@sunburypress.com.

To request one of our authors for speaking engagements or book signings, please contact Sunbury Press Publicity Dept. at publicity@sunburypress.com.

ISBN: 978-1-62006-299-9 (Trade paperback)

Library of Congress Control Number: 2019948922

FIRST SUNBURY PRESS EDITION: August 2019

Product of the United States of America
0 1 1 2 3 5 8 13 21 34 55

Set in Bookman Old Style
Designed by Crystal Devine
Cover by Lawrence Knorr
Cover photo by Mel B. Elder Jr.
Edited by Lawrence Knorr

Continue the Enlightenment!

CONTENTS

FOREWORD

CALVIN RICHARDSON is one of the most talented people that I know. He is not only a talented singer and songwriter, but I am pleased that's my brother. We first met as kids, singing gospel together in a group called Little Cedric and the Hailey Singers. Years later, we all followed our own paths—me through the group Jodeci, and him through the legendary Calvin Richardson Experience. Through it all, however, we never lost sight of the family connection. Southern roots run deep, and the soulful sounds and talent of The Calvin Richardson Experience are the personification of all our unforgettable experiences. I'm pleased that his fans get to experience how the story began and continues to evolve. This is an awesome read and an eye-opener, especially for those trying to break into the business.

Cedric "K-Ci" Hailey
Member of Legendary R&B Groups
Jodeci and K-Ci & JoJo

INTRODUCTION

OW MANY YEARS have you wasted hindering your true potential predicated upon what others think about you? Are you currently living your best life, or does it seem as if life is leaving you behind? It's true that we cannot do anything to change the past; however, we do hold the power to determine our future. Your current stage in life—age, race, status, etc.—has nothing to do with your true potential. Once you make a strong determination to *do you,* nothing or no one will be able to prevent you from taking the steps necessary to live the life that you've always wanted to experience. In other words, you begin intuitively making decisions that bring you closer to achieving your dreams or visions instead of worrying about what others will think about you. You owe it to yourself to do what brings you fulfillment, void of the misplaced opinions of those who fail to see the targets you're attempting to reach. Throughout my life, I've been forced to make some very difficult decisions that did not always sit well with those closest to me. In the

1

end, however, I could not allow myself to suffocate beneath the opinions of others or what they felt was best for me. Self-doubt is a dream killer that not only distorts your reality but also destroys your potential for success.

Whether on or off the stage, I've never been afraid to stand out in a crowd. My purpose has always been to remain true to who I am, to remain the best I could possibly be, and never transform into an impersonator. Even if I'm singing someone else's song, I must always sprinkle it with my own unique style, vibe, vocals and C. Rich swag. I don't set out to intentionally be different. I simply purpose in my heart to execute the gifts I've been given, unapologetically and as authentically as I possibly can, to create my own path, fulfill that unique purpose and leave a legacy for others to emulate but not duplicate. Everyone has a gift that they should use as a conduit to bridge the gap between present and future generations. Teach others to bring out the best in themselves, void of being dependent on the gifts of someone else to propel them to where they need to be.

Never empower others with the ability to determine your future or define your level of success. Goals, dreams, and visions last much longer than the circle of friends or family who stick around as you strive to bring your vision to fruition. Doing what's best for your own life requires focus, persistence, patience, and the ability to appreciate seasons of aloneness. Rarely does someone simply walk into your life and bless you with a handful of success. Success is earned, and the attitude that you pack for the trip determines whether you arrive at it, maintain it, or lose it. Even those who are born with a so-called silver spoon in their mouth must make an intentional effort to sustain their success and to grow their own legacy. I did not grow up with that silver spoon. I grew from very humble beginnings, but I always knew that I wanted more. Destiny constantly tugged at my self-conscious. Even when the support was absent, or my circle was small, and negativity reigned around me, my desire to succeed superseded the disappointments of having to trek this journey alone. If I'd gauged my success on my immediate surroundings, I would not have been able to retire from the 9-to-5 lifestyle at the young age of 21. The definition of success is different for everyone. Therefore, only *you* can define what it means to finally experience it. In other words, you must *"do you,"* and determine the essential parts of your existence that you refuse to relinquish to appease others. The question to ask is, *How bad do you want it?* Are you willing to do what it takes to follow your own path and essentially *"do you"* when all of *"them"* have abandoned the journey?

Music molded an attitude of excellence that drove me to go after life with an inexplicable zeal. That all-or-nothing attitude as a young boy shaped me into the man I've become. When you realize your purpose and grasp a zeal to see the vision to fruition, life begins to feel like the rush you receive from writing a hit record. You do not always know how the song will end, but you know that the message and the melody are destined to be unforgettable. My purpose remains to always teach those with dreams and visions to appreciate the wins as well as the losses. Unforgettable lessons are entangled in both outcomes, if only we take time to listen and pay attention.

Though it may often seem as if others are arriving at their destinations before we achieve our desired dreams and aspirations, we must maintain an attitude of excellence, determination, and focus that prevents us from giving up on the vision that torments us night and day. I will not say that there are no shortcuts, but I will point out that most shortcuts come with a price and force us to take more losses than we can afford in the end. Never allow a set-back to snatch your gift and lay it on a shelf of unfulfilled dreams. Pick it up, dust it off, keep moving, and gain a greater determination that you will achieve all that life has for you. Those around you will not always understand your drive and determination, but you cannot allow that to dissuade you. Your pursuit to fulfill your passion must become a relentless obligation that rules and reigns, even when there are no cheerleaders around to encourage you to keep going. The words *Do You* are a hard-core reminder that we have a responsibility to exercise the gifts we've been given despite our circle or lack thereof.

People often ask my advice on finding their gift and walking in their destiny, especially when it comes to the ins-and-outs of the music industry. I never tell people what their gift is, but I occasionally lend advice on honing their strengths and staying committed to the process. I wrote this book as a way of offering a small glimpse into the journey from humble beginnings to making a living doing what I love the most. No matter where I am or what I'm doing in life, I will always maintain a special love affair with the music. It's a huge part of who I am. It's what I do.

When purpose is deeply ingrained in the fabric of your being, you have no choice but to respond to the sound of destiny singing your name.

—C. RICH

1

IN THE BEGINNING

THE LIGHTS GLISTEN the stage in all its glory as the crowd readies themselves for a performance, their entertainment for the evening, and for some, a few hours of escape from the reality of life. Hey, I can relate. Everyone escapes to something. For me, it's the studio. For others, my music is occasionally their place of escape. I appreciate that I can be that place of peace for those who've had a long day at work, recovering from a break-up, or just needing to mellow out to some soulful sounds, which is why I always try my best to deliver a stellar performance that leaves the crowd reminiscing about The Calvin Richardson Experience!

I often unwind at the gym prior to performing and before retreating to my hotel room to choose the evening's attire. I used to be responsible for all the decisions regarding the music, the evening's attire, the technicalities of the business and so forth. As I remained committed to the gift, however, the missing components needed to take my career to the next level began coming to me.

I knew as the career progressed, the image would evolve along with the music. I'd already begun veering away from the hip urban look and more toward a style that was reflective of the audiences that I sing to on a weekly basis. As you evolve, become unstoppable, not because you don't have fears and doubts, but because you refuse to become stagnated by them. I believe that when you earnestly remain committed to the gift, then the gift gives back in the form of supplying you the necessary ingredients to fulfill its destiny.

Every decision made behind the scenes is strategic. The hat I wear, the attire, the sunglasses, the cologne, the mood. The songs of choice: always know your audience. Am I the headliner? Who are the other artists performing tonight? How much time do I have with the fans? My motto has always been, and remains, to *give the people what they want*. It's like a couple in love holding hands, intertwining their fingers like pieces of a puzzle connecting perfectly to reveal a beautiful image.

Though I find inspiration in many areas of life, when it comes to performing, the fans are my greatest inspiration. Hence, my frustration when the music is tainted, or the sound is mediocre. Though it seems as if artists simply walk onto the stage, grab the mic, and bellow out their world-renowned tunes, there's so much more the audience will never see. By the time I step onto the stage, innumerable steps have already taken place to make the moment happen. Lights. Camera. Action. But let's start at the beginning. How did I even arrive at the stage? How did I begin making a living off the God-given talent, for which I am eternally grateful? Who is Calvin Richardson, C-Rich, Mr. Monroe, the King of Hearts, the Prince of Soul?

Who knew that nestled 30 miles outside of Charlotte, North Carolina in the city of Monroe, the imaginative ingenuity of a young boy's determination would ignite the fiery inspiration of musical genius that infused his environment. Steered by the gospel sounds that loomed throughout his childhood and captivated by the smooth rhythm and blues legends that echoed so eloquently, his fortitude and commitment to learning more of this fascinating world of uninhibited expression drove him to a decision. He would not stop until he met his goal of moving the masses with his musical message. And boy, did he have a message! That young boy out of Monroe, North Carolina was me, of course. I was never able to quite shake the hunger and desire to share the sounds of expression that continually played from the depths of my soul—a place of selfless authenticity.

We originally lived in McBee, South Carolina but moved to Monroe, North Carolina when I was about six years old. I was the fifth of nine children, all crammed into a two-bedroom house with no privacy and no room for complaints. My mother and stepfather slept on one side of the living room, and my sister slept on the other side of the room. My oldest brother had his own room, while the remaining seven children stuffed themselves into one bedroom with one bed where we all curled up horizontally to sleep. You know, when people ask why I'm so humble, I honestly believe it has a lot to do with my appreciation for the things that many people take for granted. When you grow up with little, you instinctively learn not to take things or people for granted.

Needless to say, my mother ran a tight ship, but that still did not keep us from bickering and fighting with each other. With so many personalities crammed into such tight quarters, I'm sure it was a challenge to manage it all, but in the end, she still did a remarkable job. I followed my mother everywhere. I knew my real father but never had much of a relationship with him. As a child, we'd travel to McBee, South Carolina in the summer and stay with my maternal grandmother, and because the town was so small, you'd always run into someone you knew. Consequently, I'd occasionally run into my father at the corner store, but that was about the gist of our relationship.

My stepfather was in the home, but he was more of a silent fixture than a mentor or disciplinarian. Our mother, however, left little room in our lives to run the streets, as all we really knew was church. Almost seven days a week, we were either at a prayer meeting, a revival, a bible study, or regular church service. When we weren't in church, it seemed as if church came to us. There was almost always a group visiting from the church having a prayer meeting in our home. The only thing I looked forward to was singing because everything started and ended with a song. Admittedly, as I grew older, I grew tired of that church life and began retreating to various genres of music as a way to escape from what had become routine. It's why I enjoyed going to hang out with my cousins and my uncles in the summer during our visits to South Carolina. For those few moments, I was able to unapologetically enter a thrilling world of musical exploration.

I especially loved visiting my uncle J.B. He was that cool uncle who loved to let the drinks flow, party and was always fun to hang around. Then there was Uncle Troy. I loved this dude because I was just amazed by his musical talent. He could play anything: the piano, bass guitar, lead guitar, the harmonica and other instruments with such precision that I would just stand there in awe and watch him play sometimes for what seemed like hours. He had no formal training and played without any sheet music. He was amazing. Just being around him, I learned how to play musical instruments, and I can see how his musical talents rubbed off on me at an early age.

My entire family, it seemed, was musically inclined. They all sang or played instruments or belonged to a local gospel group. Hanging out with my cousins at my uncles' homes, however, allowed me the freedom to engage in unencumbered imaginative experimentation with all types of musical genres. Unlike the solely gospel environment of my home, the atmosphere at my uncles' homes was free, a total deflection from everyday life at my mother's, which drowned in Bible study, gospel music, and Jesus-only centered sentiments. I share fond memories with my cousins of playing musical instruments and having a blast singing along to the old school artists such as Bobby Womack, Sam Cooke, Al Green, Michael Jackson, and others.

Taking a break from the mundane ritual of church life was refreshing and presented an outlet to freely express the musical gifts that we were probably unaware we possessed at the time. Life is funny, however. The things we hate the most growing up are often the things that we lean on the most during the tests and trials of adulthood. Though it seemed that I sometimes strayed a bit from my gospel roots, the seeds my mother planted never died. They continued blossoming me into the man whom I've become—one passionately partaking in destiny's call. I don't have to chase it. Destiny doesn't run from us. It's right there allowing our free will to embrace it. So, I willingly walked right into it, reminding myself that along with the gift comes the sacrifice.

Consequently, I've learned to celebrate the pinnacles of life and remember the hard-core lessons taught from the places of no-return. When life makes an impromptu U-turn and fear of failure attempts to creep into my psyche, I revert to my roots, remember who I am, and the ability that I've been equipped with to overcome obstacles. The fear of failure forces us to remain in a constant cycle of false starts, what-ifs, and self-doubt. To boldly live a dream, however, is to relinquish your obstinate self-control and acquiesce to a vision that only you can see, feel, touch and almost taste.

I know all too well the disappointment of false starts and fear of unfulfilled dreams, but somehow, I've always been able to rise, dust off the disappointment, and continue living out loud the vision attached to my destiny. It's a relentless pursuit of your passion that forces you to keep going, even when it appears that the odds are against you. The mistake that people make is giving up too soon.

Life is unpredictable, and each time we feel as if we almost have it figured out, we're thrown another curveball to remind us to stay focused. The hills and valleys are not always pleasant, but if you stay the course, your travail will ultimately lead to the even plateaus and high mountaintops. It's said that it's always darkest before the break of day. The problem is that many times we give up before we can fully explore and enjoy our daybreak experiences. I am constantly reminded that whether I continue to persevere or give up, the sun will continue to overcome the darkness, and the moon will not cease to lend the light of its mystique to the sky. In other words, life continues to evolve, whether we choose to participate in it or not. It doesn't mean that we failed simply because things did not work out as planned. Oftentimes, it's God's way of showing us that we were headed down the wrong path. What seems most sensible to us is not always expedient. Triumph lives amongst your trials and tries, but you will never experience the pleasure of victory by giving up after failure. Overcome fear by facing head-on the thing that you fear the most. Remember that you cannot be replicated or duplicated, which is why the gift that you've been given must be released.

My mom introduced my brothers and me to singing when I was a kid in the church. There were five of us, and I was the youngest one in the group. I don't know how I ended up as the lead singer, but somehow it just worked out that way. My mom and grandmother and aunts were all gospel singers as well. I grew up surrounded by music and I loved performing. We were living in McBee, South Carolina and later moved to North Carolina. Life is full circle. God will place you exactly where you need to be to set on course a series of events to propel you to your destiny.

After the seeds of godliness and steadfastness were planted by my mother, I'd be blessed by a divine encounter from another angel by the name of Mrs. Anita Hailey. It all began one Sunday afternoon at Mt. Harmon Baptist Church in Pageland, South Carolina. I was 16 years old, and I'd just finished singing a solo with a quartet group locally known as the Gospel Tornadoes. I remember *vibing* back and forth with one of the most talented guitar players, Randy Hall, who was blind. With every note I sang, he had a key to match it on his strings. We were just enjoying sharing our gifts and energizing the atmosphere. Following the service, I exited the church, and a sweet lady approached me: "You have a beautiful voice," she complimented me. "I'd love to introduce you to my son who also sings in a gospel group."

Flattered that someone had truly enjoyed my gospel rendition, I responded, "OK, thank you!"

"He's Little Cedric. He sings in the gospel group, Little Cedric and the Hailey Singers."

"Really? Little Cedric is your son?" You'd have to be in the church world to understand what a big deal this was to me at the time. Cedric and his group were very well-known on the gospel scene, and for his mother, the prestigious and honorable Mrs. Anita Hailey to enjoy my singing was truly an honor because Cedric & JoJo even at their young age were considered amongst the best. The entire family was comprised of talented gospel singers. Their albums topped the Billboard gospel charts. I was ecstatic that Mrs. Hailey would allow me the opportunity to meet one of my gospel idols. I came to know them as Cedric and JoJo. I even became a member of the group Little Cedric and the Hailey Singers, but years later the world would come to know them as K-Ci and Jo-Jo of the iconic groups Jodeci, and K-Ci and Jo-Jo.

That one encounter with Mrs. Hailey changed my life forever. At the time, I'd been singing gospel at small churches for a handshake, topped off with a pat on the back, not making any money, but simply sharing the Good News through the gift of song. Meeting Cedric and Jo-Jo, however, I began singing with them at sold-out gospel concerts and packed-out churches and auditoriums. It was the first time I experienced arriving at venues with the lines already wrapped around the building. It was truly amazing! I was also in awe of the fact that we actually made money by doing what we all loved the most—singing! It intensified the flame for my love of music.

Later, Cedric and Jo-Jo decided to pursue their R&B careers. I was supposed to become the fourth member of the group, but I was newly married at the time and about to begin a family. Therefore, to honor my wife's wishes, I remained behind and opted out of the opportunity to join forces with them to pursue the dream of going to New York on a quest to secure a record deal. The rest is history. These amazing icons went on to wow the world with their amazing talent. Although that marriage did not last, I was still blessed to continue making a prominent career by doing what I love the most—inspiring others through the gift of song.

I will forever remain thankful to Mrs. Hailey and my brothers K-Ci and Jo-Jo for embracing me as one of their own and helping to set on course the destiny that I am able to experience today. I am blessed to enjoy traveling the world making a living doing what I love the most—inspiring and entertaining my wonderful fans. K-Ci and Jo-Jo were a significant catalyst for turning my desire for music as a career into a reality. They made me feel I could honestly experience success in the music business on a professional level. Because we were so close growing up, it was also a blessing for me to witness their historical success. It really inspired me to remain in the music business, because I knew that we were all bringing a unique sound to the industry.

In life, it's often necessary to start over, revamp, recompose one's plans, but it's never necessary to give up. What if I'd packed up the music and retreated to life as normal after experiencing so many false starts? Life, as I know it today, would be nonexistent. We often idolize those at the peak of their careers, but we fail to realize the mountains they had to climb to get there. Before going solo, I decided to put together a group of my own called Undacova. One of the group members sent a demo to one of the hottest Hip-Hop producers on the scene at that time—Todd Ray, a.k.a. T-Ray. The demo piqued his interest, so he asked us to visit New York to link up with some of the connections that he had with the labels. We drove to his house in New York, went into his studio and recorded a demo. He presented it to Atlantic Records, Tommy Boy, and Dreamworks. All of them gave us a meeting, which ultimately turned into an offer, but we decided to take the offer with Tommy Boy, which seemed like our first big break. The record company gave us a modest signing bonus for our pockets, a three-bedroom apartment in Brooklyn, New York and four great Members Only style jackets with the record label's name and logo on the back. "Welcome to the music game fellas," they announced. "We're gonna take care of everything! All you have to do is sing!" I later realized, however, that life is not quite that simple, especially life in the industry.

We were flying high and even had our single "Love Slave" to appear on the soundtrack for the 1995 movie *New Jersey Drive*. Out of nowhere, however, I found myself at a crossroad and facing a very difficult decision. I was approached by the label to leave the group and go solo. It was their opinion that since I was writing most of the songs and singing most of the leads, and the majority of the background vocals, then I might as well go solo and drop the group altogether. Though I knew the impact of refusing this deal, I simply could not accept it. It didn't feel right to abruptly leave the group out in the cold in such a way, so of course, I declined the offer. So, before the album got a release date, we were all eventually dropped from the label. Of course, the group was devastated by this news, and I felt helpless. I knew the terms that the label had offered me, but I also knew that even if I'd accepted the terms, they'd still dismantle the group. We all eventually went our separate ways, but because music reigned in the fabric of my being I could not go back to life as usual. Music was, and remains, my *normal.*

When your back is against the wall, you develop the fight or flight syndrome—run due to fear or stand your ground and fight for what's yours. You fight the urge to give up, fight to keep going, or avoid the issue altogether. We do not always make the correct decision the first time, so we must trek back to that same crossroad and start over until we get it or give up. Crawling into a shell and hiding does nothing to free you from the turmoil you face when trying to flee destiny. Whatever your gift, it has a unique look, sound, and voice. Music runs through my veins. I sing from the heart, so you can feel it in your soul.

In order to make a difference,
first, you have to be different!
You can't be like everyone else and
expect to change their views.

—C. RICH

2

SOULFUL SOUND

THERE'S AN IMAGE that music fans often attach to the sound and the presence of their favorite artists. Nobody in my past, when I was growing up, looked or dressed like me. For some reason, I always enjoyed being different, to set my own style, to run at my own pace. It's not that I intentionally tried to be different. In hindsight, I was creating an image for myself at a young age. Without even realizing it, this unique persona became as much of the Calvin Richardson Experience as the songs I sing or the roses I pass out at every show. We are all unique individuals, but having the courage to embrace the part of you that is different requires an attitude, which doesn't allow room for the critics to mold and shape the real *you*.

Uniqueness is a mindset, and I made up my mind long ago that I must be true to who I am. To be anything else, would stifle my growth and limit my creativity. Although, growing up, we didn't have a lot of things or clothes, I've always liked to dress well. I believed *it's not what you wear; it's how you wear it.*

My friends and family would often ask me, "Why are you all dressed up?" or "Why are you dressed in your Sunday clothes?" It's funny, but people still ask me the same thing, and my answer remains the same: *I don't need an excuse to dress well.* I refuse to dress down to fit in. Thankfully, I was never forced to dress a certain way as a youth. Now, as a parent, I believe in allowing my children to truly express their uniqueness through their gifts and talents while simultaneously being inspired by those who pave the way. Although I gained inspiration from many of the old school artists, my sole desire has always been to develop my own unique sound. When you are blessed with a gift, it carries a responsibility to use it and not trade it in for a replica. Use your weaknesses as a stepping stone to become a better version of the real *you.* Use your strengths as a guide to build your brand and create your legacy.

My strength lies in my live performances. I haven't made records all my life, but I have been singing and performing almost all my life; so, it's second nature. Even when people see me for the first time, they relate. They relate to the joy or pain that the songs I sing reflect. It causes them to reminisce on their own situations, and suddenly they realize that we're all just trying to figure out this love and life thing together. There's a connection. This is part of the reason I enjoy mingling with the people in the audience. Even if I'm not directing my attention directly toward them, they get it. They feel it. They're drawn in by it. So, in that aspect, I've been blessed. I love going into the audience and mingling with the crowd. I draw energy from their vibe and don't mind inserting myself as part of the crowd.

I become totally engrossed when I open my mouth to sing. I tap into my roots. It's a natural thing for me. There's often a moment when I'm singing that I become so immersed in the song, the music, and the lyrics, I feel a supernatural experience taking place on the stage that the audience can't see, but they can feel it! As an artist, you must give your all, regardless of the situation. I was asked once if I ever get nervous before I hit the stage or while performing. My reply was, "No. I'm always ready." I prefer going straight from the parking lot straight to the stage, only stopping for a quick prayer. I get antsy having to wait backstage too long before performing. I want to take all that built up energy and immediately release it into the music and the performance. Honestly, there's only been one time that I remember being extremely nervous. I was to perform at the Concord Motor Speedway in North Carolina. My *then* manager and I had gone over to do a soundcheck about an hour or so before it was time to perform and there were a few people milling around. One or two even stopped for a quick photo opt, which always gives me a little extra confidence. When it was showtime, I stepped on the stage and was gripped by fear. Why? Because *no one* was in the audience. The only people in attendance were the two of us . . . well three, counting the sound engineer. Now I know it sounds crazy to be nervous with no one in the crowd as opposed to feeling free and at ease amongst a crowd of hundreds of people or more, but I felt out of my element. Still, I stood there, and for thirty minutes I performed as if the audience was filled with fans. Admittedly, it was one of the hardest performances I've ever had to get through, but I never sacrificed my sound due to the circumstances. Ultimately, it's all about fulfilling your passion, doing what you love to do. For me, it's creating great music and performing.

Even in middle and high school, I'd always enter talent shows because I looked forward to sharing my gift. Even when I didn't win, I kept entering the talent shows and kept singing. Losing kept me coming back. For most people, once they win, there's nothing to fight for anymore when it comes to that particular battle. That's why the underdog is the one that you always have to watch. His motivation is different. No one sees him coming because he is often secure in who he is without boasting about what's in store. For me, at a certain point, it stopped being about winning or losing. It was all about the comeback. As an artist, you never stop honing your gift, evolving, creating, or inventing. It's just a natural inclination to push beyond the limits of your capacity. It's the only way to really see what gifts still lie dormant that need to be shared with the world.

I believe that the creativity of an individual reveals the soulish side—the true essence of who he or she really is beyond the mask. No matter how hard a person may try to hide the true essence of himself, if you allow him to express his creative side, therein you will find his authenticity. Place a paintbrush in a painter's hand and he will express life through the brilliance of the brush. Place a pen in a writer's hand and he will obsessively become engrossed with describing that picture with words. You want to know what a singer is thinking? Place a mic in his hand. Because I was raised surrounded by women—my mom, my grandmother, aunts, sister, cousins, church ladies—I learned the heartbeat of what makes women tick, and much of what I learned reflects in the music. The mystique of a woman versus her overt and candid authenticity inspired me to discuss matters of the heart through song. It's that same authenticity that entices the listener to become enthralled by the reality of the lyrics.

The song "Falling Out," for instance, was inspired by a relationship I went through while making my second album, entitled *2:35 PM*. It became so tumultuous and tiring that it literally drained me of almost all my creative energy during the process of making that album. I was forced to end it simply to salvage my peace of mind.

Another song I wrote entitled "You're So Amazing" stemmed from a relationship with a *then* good friend who was very hard-working, smart, caring, and generous—truly an amazing person who was very instrumental behind the scenes helping me through a lot of personal struggles and in rebuilding my life. And although the arrangement ended, we both knew that no matter where our lives veered in the future, that the friendship would forever remain cemented in the chronicles of our memories and experiences. Consequently, I wrote the song to pay homage, not necessarily to her or the relationship, but to so many people whose unselfish giving of themselves to others—with no expectation of anything in return—make a lasting impact, not only in someone's career but in the individual's life as well.

The song, "Can't Let Go" was inspired by a long-time, long-term, love-relationship I've been in, it seems forever. No matter how rough things get, regardless of the ups or downs we may have had, love always outweighs the faults. I felt compelled to write this one in honor of that relationship and to let her know that despite our obstacles, I simply *can't let go*; so, after writing the song, I married my beautiful wife. This song was also inspired by all of the people who've been blessed enough to find their soul mate—that one person whom they feel was specifically created to click and bond with them and bring out the best of who they are ("Like my legs, I can't walk around without you!). Inspired by the same long-term relationship. I co-wrote another song, along with Kenny "Babyface" Edmonds. Babyface is just an incredible lyricist who can write about any subject and make it incredible. But that song landed on the album of Mr. Charlie Wilson. The song was released in 2009 and was titled "There Goes

My Baby." It went on to top the Billboard charts and was nominated for a Grammy Award for Best Male R&B Vocal Performance. I earnestly believe that if you become vulnerable enough to allow your authenticity to shine while exercising your gift, then it will automatically attract success. Despite the negative influences that attempt to deter you, walk in your calling and your gift will make room for you.

Every opportunity you get to share your gift, do it willingly and have fun. Enjoy the moment. As an entertainer, people pay to see you, but they often wish that they were the ones being paid to be seen, so remain grateful and humble for the opportunities that you've been given. You don't always get what you deserve; you get what you work hard for. The businessman is the part of myself that I learned to become. I realized some time ago that the music game and the music business are two totally different things. The music game is the art of making people believe you're something that you're not. The business is the work you must do behind the scenes that keeps you *on* the scene. So, don't wish me luck on the business. Wish me well in my career, because if I stay true to myself, handle my business, and work harder than I play, I'll never need any luck. I'm today's keeper of yesterday's soul music, which is why I'm very intentional about the decisions I make when writing the music and the business side of my career. Sometimes you must change for the better to initiate growth. However, I still stay true to my sound. I am who I am, and I desire that same consistency to continue being revealed through my music.

Therefore, I try to use wisdom when it comes to the music as well as the brand. If I only have one show in a small club or cafe, I'm going to go out there and give the fans a memorable experience. I don't reserve anything for the next show. I sing from the heart and soul even if I'm serenading one woman. However, I do take time, like most artists, to allow my voice to recover. Many times, I've struggled through an entire concert, singing my heart out, losing my voice, but the fans take that ride with me because they've come to know that sometimes the struggle makes the experience. It's tough to sing nonstop and then go into the studio without a voice. So, I've learned to block off time and allow my voice rest to ensure that when I get into the studio that I can make that record.

Many young artists enter the business with stars in their eyes, but in doing so, they become blinded by the business. You can't stop working on yourself and the music simply because you're signed by a label. Actually, you must work that much harder and be willing to out-work those who are working for you. The label should go to sleep long before you retire for the night. As a young artist, it took me a while to figure this out, but when I got it, I've been going strong ever since. Upcoming artists often ask me if it's difficult to break into the business. The answer to this question has changed throughout the years simply because of how much technology has evolved. When I was a young artist, it was much more difficult. We literally had to drop tracks in the mail and drive long distances for an opportunity to meet the right people. It was all about that one-on-one interaction where you had to hustle and grind to be at the right place at the right time amongst the right people, and so forth. In today's social media age, however, there's greater access. This means essentially that the world is yours. You simply just need to remain persistent, continue to hone your craft and build your audience. Out-work those who are working to help you succeed. Achieve beyond those who are working against your success. Often, it's all about timing. You will not always understand why you meet certain people. Life, however, is full circle, and if you trust the process it will eventually lead you into the path of the right people at the right time.

I remember my first time meeting musical icon, Heavy D. When we were working on the *Undacova* album, Heavy D was working on Monifa's first album; so he'd occasionally stick his head in the studio to listen to us recording. He called me out one day and asked if I was interested in doing a solo album. That was during the time he'd just replaced Andre Harrell at Uptown Records. I declined the offer because, of course, I was still with the group and we were already signed to a label. But shortly after the group dissolved, Damian Blyden (Deo), Heavy's good friend and co-manager ran into me one night at Justin's, which was Puffy's restaurant in New York City, and extended the offer again, "Look man, we can give you this solo deal if you want it." So, I took the deal.

When I signed with Uptown, Heavy D was already working with Soul 4 Real, McGruff, The Lost Boys, and his own album. Eventually, Universal decided, for whatever reason, to pull the plug on the Uptown label and that is how I ended up with Universal. We started on the album in 1996 and finally, in 1999, we released a single. During that time, the rapper Nelly, who was on the same label had recorded his chart-topping album, and that album alone was the label's priority. Once the albums were released, it was a huge success, and although I was still on the label, all focus shifted to his project. I was not a priority at that time. It's the nature of the business. So, I always tell upcoming artists that you have to be willing to put in the work, even when you're frustrated, or things don't seem to go your way. If you're committed to the gift, you must be equally committed to the work required to share that gift with others.

In 2001, the label informed me that they wanted to record a single instead of doing a full album. Basically, they wanted to know how successful the single would be before putting an entire recording budget which at that time was $350,000 into a full album. I decided I didn't want to do that, but I did go in the studio and record a song with Eddie F and Darren Lighty called "More Than a Woman." When the label decided they just wanted to move forward with that song, I was like, "Naw, that wasn't my deal." So, with my lawyer's help, I left Universal. As fate would have it, because of "More Than a Woman," Hollywood Records came knocking around 2002. Then Angie Stone called. She'd heard "More Than a Woman," played for her by Eddie F and she invited me to come to record the song with her on her album. So, it actually came out on her album, *Mahogany Soul*, before it released on mine.

I signed a deal with Hollywood Records—one of the biggest deals I'd ever signed—and recorded my second album. It was titled *2:35 PM*, the time that my son was born. That album came out in 2003. We released "Keep On Pushing" as the single for that album, and the record did really well. We put the single "More Than a Woman" on the *Deliver Us from Eva* soundtrack (the movie with Gabrielle Union and L. L. Cool J). Shortly after, I went on what should have been a twenty-nine-city tour with Nelly and The St. Lunatics. It was a hip-hop crowd, but I was opening with my soulful sound. We ended up doing about fifteen cities before the tour was cut short.

In 2004, the label wanted me to come off the road and get back into the studio and start on my third album, which really didn't make sense to me because the ball had just started rolling. So, they enlisted Babyface as executive producer for that second album with Hollywood Records. Babyface and I created some phenomenal music, but unfortunately, we never put any of that music out except "There Goes My Baby" (sang by Charlie Wilson). That was some of the greatest material that I've ever recorded, to date. That's when Babyface was going through the separation from his wife, unbeknownst to anyone, but it was taking a long time for us to get the project completed. Hollywood Records decided to pull out. So, in

2005 I found myself out the door again without a label. At that point, I was like, *You know what, I'm gonna just chill out.* I'd already signed a lucrative publishing deal at Hollywood records. So, I just kind of walked away from the industry for a while. I bought my own studio, and I and my closest friends would just go there, hang out, party, chill, and so forth.

I remember when I was going through that stage in life, I refused to go around my mother that much. Of course, I would visit, but *not* often, and the visits were very short. She was, and remains, a very spiritual woman, not to mention that she and I were always very close. Therefore, I knew if I'd stuck around her too long, she'd immediately sense that something was off, and I'd feel ashamed. She'd know that I was partying, squandering my earnings, and veering completely away from all that she'd taught me when it comes to survival. I wasn't praying very much at the time, nor was I doing much to change my situation. For the moment, I just wanted to party the shame and disappointment away—to live free of the responsibility of life, to do my own thing, though it was the wrong thing *to do* at the time.

Life moves you like a song. You either dance to the music or change the tune. Either way, the decisions you make hold the power to change the course of your situation, make it worse, or maintain until you receive an answer to the problem. When I'm displeased with how life is unveiling my story, I write my own script and unleash the storyline through the lyrics. The studio is where I release it all and let it go.

I was once asked to describe the process I go through before going into the studio to record, to which I responded, "I just do it." My goal is to express through song the various stories I see, which is why the songs I write sometimes land on the albums of other artists; nonetheless, the story remains the same. I can honestly say that I do not have a specific ritual that I go through before creating music, because I consider life in general and the world around me inspiration. I see music in almost everything: the couple walking hand in hand, the sun peeking through the clouds after a rainy day, a broken heart, a heart in love, people dancing and enjoying life, a couple at odds with each other . . . you get the point. Music is alive in all things, and I make it almost tangible by pouring my heart and soul into my musical expression. I glean inspiration not only from my own life but from the lives of others as well.

For instance, the song I released in 2008 entitled, "She's Hurting," was inspired by a woman I knew who'd experienced heartbreak and was having a rough time dealing with it. Living in the south, we'd frequent little hole-in-the-wall joints known as Liquor Houses. These were actual residences where people would go to escape from their life for a few hours or just a few minutes and buy liquor and mingle. We were at one of these places one night and she sat there drinking the entire night to numb the pain of her aching heart. As she sat drinking the pain away with tears streaming uncontrollably down her cheeks, I wondered, *What type of pain did she just experience that led her here to release the agony this way in a public place?* It made me think of the pain that we all often go through and how we cope. We either tuck it away, release it, or deal with it head-on. Nobody likes to cry, but crying is good sometimes. Tears feel better coming out than when you're holding them in. As soon as you allow yourself to cry, healing begins. It's what allows some people to release inwardly what they're unable to express outwardly. For me, it's a no-brainer to unleash my inward thoughts in the studio. Even when something pleasant is going on in my life and I feel the need to celebrate, I do it best through song.

Whether I'm celebrating the beauty found in a woman's essence or agonizing over the heartbreak she just caused, the passion in which I deliver the song remains the same because ultimately music is always relaying a story to its audience. It's what causes some of my biggest fans to remain loyal listeners throughout the years. It's that part of me that humanizes the artist and allows the listeners to live out the song because in many instances I'm singing about an occasion in life that we have all experienced in the past or that we're currently experiencing—hence, The Calvin Richardson Experience. I call what I do an *experience* because that is ultimately what I'm expressing—various experiences from all walks of life. Everyone has his or her own coping mechanisms. If you listen carefully, you will notice that every song tells a story or shares an experience. Your experiences in life mold and shape your authenticity. Never despise your uniqueness. Never discount your experiences. They're leading you to a place of destiny that can only be occupied by your imitable presence.

During my sabbatical from the business, people kept reaching out to me wanting to know when I was going to release another album. So, after five years, I decided that maybe it was time for me to put out some more music. In 2007, Randall Grass, of Shanachie Entertainment, reached out to me regarding signing with the company. After three months, going back and forth, I signed, and we released an album in 2008 called *When Love Comes*.

It was refreshing to have complete creative control (and a little more control of the money). The difference, however, is that they targeted more of a web-based fan base, but for me, radio is the number one way to build your fan base. The album did just ok, but on the second album, I decided to spend my own money to market and promote myself more, focusing on radio exposure that I really wanted. As I stated before, you never let the label out-work you as an artist. When it's your vision, you do what it takes to make your vision a reality.

In 2009, I was approached to record a remake for the Bobby Womack album. This was an amazing honor, unbeknownst to me or the label, it was also during the time that Bobby Womack was being inducted into the Rock and Roll Hall of Fame. The album was titled *The Facts of Life*. I sang some of Bobby Womack's greatest hits, and two of the songs from my remake album were nominated for Grammys. Ann Nesby and I did a song called, "Love Has Finally Come at Last," and then there was "A Woman's Gotta Have It." Both of those songs were nominated. "Love Has Finally Come At Last" with Anne Nesby was nominated for Best Duo Vocal Performance and "A Woman's Gotta Have It" was nominated for Best Traditional Male Vocal Performance.

The skepticism surrounding the Bobby Womack remake was the fact that remake albums don't really do well. But thankfully, that's not how it turned out in this case. Although I was reluctant to record the album at first, the album was a success. My reluctance came from the responsibility of being able to represent this notable icon with the excellence he deserved. It's one thing to record one of the artist's songs, but to record an entire album of his work adds the pressure of making sure that I honored his music in the manner it deserved. Consequently, I channeled my inner Bobby Womack and got as close to his sound as I could possibly get. I think when you stay close to the remake, it's more successful than veering too far from the original to do your own thing. Of course, I added a bit of my own Calvin Richardson flare to it, but I stayed as close to Bobby Womack's original voice as possible. The single, "A Woman's Gotta Have It," especially, got a lot of radio play.

Before the album was released, it was submitted to Bobby Womack to get his seal of approval, and in the end, he loved it, so that was a great honor for me. Since we'd had such success with that album, the label was like, "Let's go for another one!" So we did!

All the songs were brand new, and with the live band playing, it was electrifying. Live music delivers a different type of vibe. If I'm really into it, it should only take a couple of hours to complete the song. I don't write anything down. I come up with a hook line and fit it to the music. I sing with my guitar and develop a melody. I then connect with musicians who are more skilled than I am in the area to take it to the next level.

Regardless of your gift, you must always know who you are and what your contributions are going to be, especially in this music industry. You can't go in trying to be the next replica of someone else. No one can be a better version of *you*. I honestly believe it's that underlying authenticity that attracts fans to the Calvin Richardson sound. My unwillingness to compromise who I am unknowingly touches the fans in an area that drives their own commitment to self-truth. People send me music to critique all the time. But I'm not a critic of people's music. I just give them advice based on my own experience.

Regardless of which bed of music I lay the message on, it remains the same—good vibes, love stories, and personal experiences. The tempo of the album must set the tone of the mood. I want to be able to entertain in an intimate setting. I don't care if it's fifty people or as few as one. I want the sound to be so precise and clear that we don't always need an amplifier, and the music doesn't have to be that loud for you to get it. One of Prince's albums was simply just his piano and his voice. That is the soulish sound that I often enjoy creating when it comes to my guitar and my voice.

My very first song, when I went solo, was an *acoustic* song. My producer wanted me to remain in that same vein, but I didn't want to be limited to just that. I kind of rebelled against it because I wanted to make a larger sound. Many years later, here I am—getting back to the essence of who Calvin Richardson is. I'm a voice. Beyond the voice, I want the listeners to hear what I'm trying to say. I don't want them to be distracted by a large band, or sound because it takes away from the message of the song, and I don't want them to miss it. I'm just trying to center everything back to me.

Though it was definitely difficult breaking into the business, it was worth it. Since my first album came out in 1999, my priorities have changed through growth and greater understanding. Sometimes I'm a headliner during the shows and sometimes I open for someone else. There will always be a caliber of artists who are considered bigger or smaller. In the interim, however, I built my brand, which wasn't easy to do. I had to find my way and prioritize my sound, my image—my brand. To me, there's nothing bigger than that.

When you first sign to a label, in your mind, you think that the label is going to make you a star. I'm not saying that's not true, but that's not how it works. The record label is a vehicle, but realistically, you have to work harder for yourself than they want to work for you. Some artists start out doing everything the label asks them to do, while others go in and challenge most of the things they're asked to do. As a result, the label gets aggravated and shelves their albums. Everything that they asked of me, I was willing to do, except compromise my sound. At the same time, however, they have budgets, and they have other priorities, which can cause your sound to be compromised, especially if it's being produced by producers brought in by the record company. It's a business. Still, it's often hard to desensitize, but you can't take everything personally. I don't allow the business side to compromise the integrity of the music. I'm grateful for the recognition that I have. I'm still here and hope to be here years from now because I decided early to put in the work to build the Calvin Richardson brand along with maintaining my soulful sound.

The industry is inundated with talented artists, especially in my native home of Charlotte, North Carolina where many talented artists were born and still reside. It's a competitive business, but you cannot blame one's failure to succeed in the industry on those who've paved the way and made a name for themselves. There is a distinct difference between the music game and the music business. I've been doing this for over two decades and it's not an easy or quick industry to break into. Even after getting a contract, you still have to make an intentional effort to promote yourself, to hone your craft, and to remain relevant. My native home of Charlotte, North Carolina is in the top ten when it comes to the music business—the talent, state-of-the-art studios, clubs, promoters, producers, radio stations, and so forth. Still, you can't negate the other side of the industry, which includes managers, attorneys, including entertainment law. A manager is like a coach. He or she is supposed to have a better view of the game—the business—than the artist, including knowledge and established relationships from which the artist can directly benefit. It requires a lot of work, dedication, and an extreme level of commitment to the artist's career, including personal and financial matters that most will not or are not willing to make. I've had a few managers throughout my career, but I've never had one who was able to do much to impact my career or assist in music matters, other than just dealing with the things that I didn't want to deal with. Most of the hometown artists—including myself—had to leave our hometowns to get to that next level and succeed. The radio stations were not playing our music. Still, despite all those obstacles, I've had songs amongst the top twenty songs on the Billboard charts others that have been nominated for Grammys. My music is being played at radio stations in major cities all over the country, but my home city isn't one of them. That's the business that's failing our Carolina artists. Aspiring artists sometimes blame the few of us who have succeeded for not helping them to succeed. The truth of the matter is that we all had to put in years of hard work before we could even think about enjoying the level of success we're experiencing today. So, it's not right to point a finger at the handful of us who've worked for decades representing, not only the Carolinas but paving the way for all the young new talent to get that next level.

Early in my career, I could identify who Calvin Richardson actually is and break into the industry without any of the artists of that time "putting-me-on" so to speak. As close as K-Ci and Jo-Jo were to me, I had no expectations of them, and I never asked them to help me. I got *in and on* by doing my own thing. On my first album, I worked with several producers who were trying to find the sound, but eventually, they had to come back to the source, *me,* and allow me to be true to who I am. I guess when you grow up surrounded by music you kind of develop a sense of what fits with you as an individual. So, my music always dabbles in my roots and who I am as an individual. The music makes you feel a certain groove, while the lyrics set the tone of the mood. That's soul music. It always delivers a mood and a message.

The first record that I owned was by the Gap Band— *Burn Rubber.* Listening to lyricists such as Charlie Wilson was inspiring. Then, there were the other greats like Bobby Womack, Marvin Gaye, Al Green and so forth. Coming from the south in North Carolina, we referred to those iconic sounds as Fish Fry music and it could always be heard playing in the background at family functions, cookouts, and other celebratory events, and parties.

My versatility in being able to work the Blues, R&B, and Soul market is that I was blessed to be able to connect with a lot of those living legends before they passed away. I think as an artist it's important to have an actual connection to your roots. So instead of just knowing who these guys are, I was able to actually speak, get advice from them, learn from them, and build relationships with them that help to strengthen the foundation upon which I was already built.

Part of being able to secure my sound is living by my own standards instead of the music industry's standards. At the end of the day, I am just an ordinary guy who happens to be in the music industry. I'm a soul singer who doesn't believe in bowing to the rules and sacrificing the sound. My motivation comes from the fact that I love what I do and I love people who have their own unique way of doing things. It drives me to keep going and to keep getting better and better. So, when I hear the fans say that my music helped them to get over a bad break up or to cheer them up or strive for more, that also inspires me to stay true to who I am.

On the opposite side of the spectrum, your music must be authentic enough to let those who've failed know that you're not perfect. I speak a lot about relationships in my songs because I've been in several where many of the breakups were due to my own shortcomings. That vulnerability in sharing the truth as an artist is what makes great music. You're not just talking about other people's experiences, but many times you're journaling your own life through the music. When I made the decision to be a writer and entertainer, that made me an open book. Singing is what I do; it's like breathing for me. The writing aspect of my career is something that I tapped into later. At the end of the day, it has to be about loving what you do and sharing the gift as opposed to being famous. I think many new artists stall because they are too focused on chasing the dream of stardom instead of focusing on the impact they could have by just being true to who they are and using their gift for the benefit of the people who support them as artists. I live by the motto of not simply waiting on things to happen, I *make* things happen. Believing is simply just not enough. *You gotta put the work in.* Even when I write a song, I try to never get too attached to it, because that song I'm writing could end up on another artist's album.

I learned that people are going through real things in their lives, so there's always a place in their hearts for someone who speaks on real issues and tells the truth. My mother always told me that what comes from the heart goes to the heart. There's always a connection between two sources that reign from a place of sincerity and authenticity. If I release what I really feel, it will mean something to those who hear it as well.

The tides of the industry change rapidly, but I remain determined to stay true to my sound. Many times, when record labels want a certain sound they will bring in producers to create it through you, but that's not who I am. I don't want to be produced to sound like someone else. I am Calvin Richardson, and I have to remain true to that sound. I have a great appreciation for being surrounded by those who enhance the unique creativity instead of trying to quench it. The freedom to remain uninhibited by a synthetic sound that bears no semblance to my character is a must if I am to remain effective and relate to those who connect with who I am as an artist. It's one of the reasons I'm able to celebrate such successful albums as, *I Am Calvin,* which I released through Eric Benet's label, Jordon House Records in 2014.

I met Eric Benet in 2013 when we were in Memphis, Tennessee at the Sisterhood Showcase. Eric had called me a few weeks prior to that and introduced me to the possibility of signing to his label, Jordan House Records. After my performance, he came backstage and introduced himself formally. He revealed that he'd just started his own record label, and I was one of the artists that he was interested in signing. He was interested in signing artists whom he'd been a fan of in the past. That was a great compliment because I had been a fan of the Eric Benet sound for years as well.

"I don't know if you are signed to anyone or if you're even free to do it, but you were the first artist that I wanted to approach when I started the label," he explained. How cool is that? His talent is phenomenal, but we'd never done any shows together and our paths never crossed. The difference between Eric's label in comparison to other labels I had previously joined was that my project was a priority. And although Eric was involved, he stilled allowed me to have creative control. He allowed me to be *me*, and that was important. I remember taking a drive with Eric, and he asked me what type of album I wanted to make. I told him something current that was still in my genre, and I wanted to make something that was sexy, yet maintained quality and substance. So, he said that they'd bring me the music and just let me vibe with it. I could say anything that I wanted to say on the record. If anything needed to be revised or scaled back, then they'd deal with it at that point. I listened to the music, expressed what I felt through song, and then Eric came in and tweaked it. In essence, that's how the album *I Am Calvin* was birthed.

If you're an artist struggling to discover who you are, dig deep and find your original sound. Once you find it, stay true to that. Receiving advice is prudent when it comes from a source of experience and authenticity, but never become something that you're not. In doing so, you become more focused on keeping up the façade than perfecting the gift.

"*In* the midst of the pouring rain, all molecular misfits of the atmosphere are purified. Like all the hurt and pain of life's strains are removed from the body of a beautiful woman through every tear held back that she don't cry. Your eyes are like heaven's window panes with the strength of an athlete, with a touch so gently brought mighty, mighty Hercules to his knees. God told Adam no, Eve made him say yes, yes. Her smell so sweet; her body waves so unique, makes a man complete. Surely, I'll eat for just one more taste of your nectar. Please don't leave."

—Love, C. RICH

3

SUBLIMINAL SEDUCTION

LIKEN MUSIC TO subliminal seduction. Allow me to explain. Music is a form of subconscious persuasion that allows the listener to travel through time and space, ponder choices, make decisions, and for the moment, even escape reality when needed. It's like a man and a woman who meet for the first time, but it seems as if they've known each other forever. They speak with their eyes and emotions without uttering verbally what they're both thinking. The chemistry is setting ablaze the desires of the heart. Whether they act on those emotions or ignore them, the silent language remains an unspoken mystery that only the two of them comprehend. It is magnetic, an almost magical unspoken language, experienced only by the two individuals—unintelligible lyrics to outsiders.

This same scenario often happens when people listen to music that draws them in, and they find themselves placing a song on repeat and listening to it for hours. It affects them in a way that's incomprehensible to outsiders. The person has become enraptured, captivated by an experience that the song unleashed, a memory provoked. Another person can enter the room and hear the same song yet remain unaffected. Music holds the power to affect our decision-making process. It can place us in a good mood when we're feeling down, or even set the mood when we need to invoke a romantic atmosphere. It can also have the opposite effect by invoking anger. Have you ever heard a song on the radio and immediately changed the channel because it provoked a nerve in you that could potentially alter your entire mood? That's the power of music—subliminal seduction.

I'm often approached by fans who express to me how moved they are by my music. I remain eternally grateful to them for sharing their many stories with me, as it inspires me to remain true to who I am and my purpose. It reminds me that as an artist I have a responsibility to avoid seemingly reckless lyrics and petty propaganda. Years ago, I remember going into the studio in my home and recording a song. I really just needed to release some things that were heavy on my mind and bothering me at the time. By the time I finished expressing myself, I'd recorded an entire single. The song was basically regarding the topic of infidelity. I worried that I was somehow doomed by my biological father's curse of unfaithfulness—never being satisfied with just one woman. I was young, and as I began to mature, I wanted to make better choices in life. However, I knew that he was in my DNA, and the struggle of growing mentally from a boy to a man would not be an easy task to tackle. I was my father's seed, but I absolutely did not want to grow that part of him that he struggled to conquer. So, instead of tormenting myself about it, I released it the only way I knew how—by recording a song. The lyrics of the song talked about my uncertainty of ever being strong enough to be faithful. I wasn't glorifying disloyalty, but I simply needed an outlet to express my fear of failure.

I was up all night in the studio recording this particular song. So, when my girlfriend at the time, got up to get ready for work and realized I never came to bed, she came into the studio where she knew I'd be.

"What are you working on?" she asked.

"I recorded a new song," I explained.

"Can I hear it?" I was a little reluctant knowing that she, of all people, focused on the lyrics of the songs that I'd write more than any other element.

"Sure."

I played the song, and by the time the first verse was over—midway through the first hook—she was in tears. Her personal response caught me off guard, and I immediately felt regret. I never released that song, because it is never my intention to have that negative effect on the women who listen to my music. I simply feel as an artist that I hold a responsibility to inspire positive change, or in the least, just allow the fans to listen to good, fun music that invokes happiness—something they can dance to, and for a few minutes cast away their cares. Although it was simply my mode of artistic expression, I never want to appear that I am glorifying a negative side of manhood that brings others pain. Perhaps one day I will release that song, but for now, it remains archived safely amongst other unreleased stories I've recorded throughout the years.

I honestly enjoy the fact that my listeners choose my music to wind down after a grueling day. The fans often share stories of pulling into their driveway after a long day at work and just sitting in the car listening to and enjoying the entire album before getting out of the car. Some express that they've felt torment over how to end a bad relationship, but after listening to my music, it gave them hope and courage to simply do what needed to be done. Others reveal the hope and inspiration they hear in the lyrics—of someday finding their soulmate, void of all the unnecessary drama that accompanies toxic relationships, and so forth.

Life is too short to live in a bubble of uncertainty. When you find your mind drifting off to certain lyrics, the question to ask yourself is, *Why?* What is it about the words that hypnotize you and causes your out-of-body experiences, plummeting you into a world of daydreaming about what *could-be*? Are you living your life or sacrificing your own happiness to fulfill the dreams and visions of someone else? It's only when you begin to "do you" that you will be able to live the life that you daydream about daily. That's one of the reminders that I want to always deliver through the lyrics to the listeners—*do you!*

I often hear fans upset because they feel my music is underrated—that it doesn't get enough radio play, or in their opinion, there are still too many people out there who have never heard of me. I understand their frustration because I know that they relate to the music from a personal level. I appreciate that they've been willingly seduced by and support the sound. However, people who truly know what I do, don't necessarily underrate me. On the business side, it's all about promoting. If you have a product out there—in my case an album—that people don't know about, you're not going to be able to sell a number significant enough to be considered successful.

Ultimately, I feel that as long as the music continues to move you in a certain way and makes my world go around, then I've achieved my goal as an artist. When you are passionate about your craft, you should never allow others to believe in you more than you believe in yourself. Once you find your voice or your niche and become comfortable with who you are, you become unstoppable because your steps are already ordered. I am inspired by everyday life, which makes it easy for me to continue pulling fans into the world of hope through sound.

For instance, the fans always express to me how my music either helped them to recover from a break-up or inspired them to make-up and even stay together, realizing that "everything changes, even the seasons" (lyrics from the single, "Falling Out"). If it's love, it's worth the stay. Relationships are like music. We either vibe to the beat and turn up the volume or change the channel when the chemistry is nonexistent. I pause to talk about relationships for a moment because I, unfortunately, learned the hard way not to underestimate the complexity of a solid union or overestimate the simplicity of what's required to produce your own magical beat.

I can honestly say that I've only had my heart broken one time. I was in high school when I found out that my girlfriend at the time, my first love, was cheating on me with her best friend, a guy whom she hung around often. I was devastated. The memory of that incident made it hard for me to trust in a relationship. My outlook was, *if I can't see you, I don't know what you're doing, and you don't know what I'm doing.* After that painful incident, I began being unfaithful and not giving my all. I unfortunately also transferred those feelings of mistrust into my business relationships and to other acquaintances. It made me understand the importance of healing before moving on. I learned a lot about myself: my strengths, weaknesses. It's difficult to hide my true emotions, so they often spill out of me into the lyrics. Or when I'm performing, the audience is often experiencing a myriad of emotions that I simply cannot hide, nor do I try to hide them. I honor those many experiences by releasing my story onto the stage.

Women often share with me that I make them feel as if we are the only two people in the room, even when it's filled with others. I never intentionally sought out to have that gift. I just try to remain kind and to be true to myself and who I am as a person, not just as an artist. I think what they're experiencing during those pivotal moments is me releasing my truth . . . a truth to which many of them can relate. We're often forced to take the good with the bad, but the tricky part is maintaining the good in yourself while overcoming all the bad experiences. In other words, don't become bitter and don't become stuck. Those are the types of things that not only hinder you from finding true love, but they also form a ceiling on your career due to a lack of distrust.

Just like every woman is different, every relationship is different. The danger is taking the old mindset into the new relationship and making the new person a subject for the acts of those who disappointed us in the past. I think that while women become fascinated with the possibility of love, men are not always swayed by that same motivation. It doesn't mean anything is wrong with her as an individual when men don't fall in love so easily. Some things, such as love, take time to fully develop and just can't be forced. Sometimes if a man is not ready to totally commit, he will do just enough to keep her, but not enough to completely give in to a commitment. Been there. Done that. So, I always tell the ladies, *If he is showing you his truth, don't try to twist it into a lie to make yourself feel better.* Likewise, if you're listening to a lie, don't try to dress it up as truth. Seeing is believing. Two good people could still make a bad relationship if the relationship is being forced simply to appease one person. Life is too short for all that if you're not married. Married couples fall in and out of love all the time, but it takes discipline to remain committed to the relationship long enough for the love to return. But if you're not married and simply seeking Mr. Right, *do you!* In other words, stop giving all of you to people who drain your love and take your kindness and generosity for granted. Otherwise, you will become bitter and unattractive to the next good person who has nothing to do with the wrongdoings of the ones who preceded them.

The same goes for the fellas. Don't prolong the inevitable and risk ruining someone. It's better for her to go through a little pain now and get over it than to allow her to go all in and then you bounce.

"Pain is such a funny thing. 'Cause when it hurts, it hurts, but when it leaves, it goes. So it's better to hurt a little bit now than to be so far gone and hurt a whole lot tomorrow." (Lyrics from Looks Like You've Been Crying)

In case you're wondering where the inspiration for many of my love songs comes from, it's real life. I've hurt some and some have hurt me in return. Through the lyrics, I release it all, expressing real life, and let it go. Still doesn't make it easy. Though it seems like men get over a break-up easier than women, they're actually just moving on to dull the pain. So, before they can even heal, truth is, they're taking that baggage on to the next relationship without taking time to totally let go of the first. For many men, the best way to get over one woman is to move on to the next one. It's often easier for a woman to give her heart to someone. For men, however, it takes a little longer. So when he does finally give in to love and his heart is broken, everyone after that pays the price by his hesitancy to give his all to the relationship, simply because he's scared of being hurt again. It often takes men longer than women realize to recover from heartbreak; so even when it seems like we've moved on, we really haven't. We just switched partners.

I think love can be so obsessive that if you're not careful you will lose yourself trying to salvage something that disintegrated a long time ago. I remember accidentally being caught up in a love triangle. I rode with a friend of mine to visit his female friend. As we were standing outside, I noticed another man walk up and kind of size me up. Being from the streets, I knew the look. I didn't know that the disgruntled look was about a woman, but I knew the look of resentment. Although I knew who he was, we didn't know each other like that, so I didn't say anything to him. I just returned the gaze with a look like, *What's up?* Possessed by jealousy, he reached for his waist, took out his gun, and I heard a loud, *pop!* Then I realized that he'd shot me in my leg and ran off. As it turned out, he was the ex-boyfriend of the lady my friend was there to visit. Since I had a reputation of having a few lady friends, he erroneously assumed that I was there to see her, but I wasn't. Obsessive love gets crazy *real* quick. He could have killed me that day, all over a misunderstanding, because he was blinded by a toxic, obsessive type of emotion that drove him over the edge. When forced, it's no longer love, but instead, control.

"Sometimes, love can be so cruel. Spinning 'round and 'round, nothing left to hold onto. Other times, love can be untrue. I'll keep this feeling deep inside, 'cause girl I still want you."

This is a verse from my song "Never Knew Love," but it's so real. How many times have we tried to suppress feelings that we shouldn't possess for someone? The heart wants what the heart wants, but the mind is there to remind the heart *not* to be selfish. We can't always have what we want, so we must make some grown-up decisions and move on. We don't forget about the person, but we must just file away the memories in a compartment that's not allowed to be touched any longer. Hence, the lyrics, ". . . sometimes love can be so cruel . . ." I think this is what draws listeners to the lyrics of this song and other songs like it. It's the reality of life that causes us to travel through space and time, daydreaming while the music is blaring in the background. We become so engrossed in the lyrics that while we're physically standing in the middle of the kitchen, our mind has traveled hundreds of miles away. We begin thinking about the person, wondering what he or she is doing at that very moment or living out our fantasy with the individual in the form of *what-ifs*. I'm blessed to be able to remind the listeners to never take love for granted.

In my opinion, there's no such thing as real love or fake love. Love is love all by itself. Either it's *love* or it isn't. Ultimately, even in bad times, the thing that holds the relationship together is mutual respect, understanding, and communication. If you have respect for each other, it dictates how you communicate with each other. I learned the hard way that I must always be considerate and implement selflessness into the relationship versus selfishness. I used to have a very dismissiveness attitude in my relationships. If I didn't want to talk about an issue or deal with it, I just shut down and shut her out. So, in relationships, I think we have to make a conscious effort not to hold on to our ego so tightly that we push away the other person unintentionally. There is no pride in love. Every woman wants to be treated right but so does the man. Each person must make the other a priority; otherwise, the relationship begins draining the life out of you very quickly. Know your boundaries and deal-breakers.

For me, I always had to wait for someone who understood the priority of music in my life. Without music, I don't function at full capacity. That's something that can often be difficult to explain. It can also be something that's impossible for some women to deal with. I get it, but at the same time, giving up the music was never an option for me. I think every person wants to find that special individual that they can vibe with, call their own, and just enjoy as the love of their life, but these things should never be forced or rushed. It never ends well when relationships are birthed out of desperation. Don't allow loneliness to pull you into a full-blown relationship with someone who is just passing through. In their quest to "do them" don't allow them to *do you* in such a negative way that you're left wandering blindly in a state of brokenness and bitterness.

I'm not only a singer and entertainer but also a songwriter. Many of the songs I sing evolve from my own mistakes. Still, when I sing things like, *Treat Her Right . . . make her feel special*, there's always someone who takes the lyrics negatively or personally as if I'm chastising men in an area in which I have no right. The lyrics don't chastise. They educate and encourage with the truth so that others who might be in danger of losing the one person who matters to them the most have a chance to stop and think for a moment before destroying something that they may never be able to get back again. In the streets they say, don't hate the player, hate the game. But I say, put away the hate and the games altogether and focus on the love before you lose it.

That's the wonderful thing about music and entertainment. I can please the fans while simultaneously moving the crowd with the truth in song. It may seem as if I'm always catering to the women. I guess in a way I am because a woman raised me. Women were very instrumental in steering me in the direction that I needed to go. I understand, however, that women are not always right, which is why I tell the guys if you're in a relationship with someone who does not appreciate you or drains you instead of building you up, then you need to do your own self-evaluation to find out why you're holding on to something that's not holding on to you and what are you getting out of it.

To compromise your own happiness is to devalue portions of your life that you can never get back. To find someone who complements the part of you that drives your passion instead of stifling and debasing your creativity is a gift to never take for granted. When you sing certain lyrics, no questions are asked, and no explanation is needed:

"Like my legs, I can't walk around without you. Like my heart, the rhythm's bound to change without you, the way it beats, tapping on my mind., when I think about you girl, holdin' on I can't let go of you."

I think that everyone wants to be in love, even if they're afraid of it. The reason these lyrics are so relatable is that it's something that we all long for, and if we've already found it, then we fight to keep it. Essentially, as an artist, you want to reach beyond the surface and dig deep into the soul of the message that you want to relay to the audience. If it feels watered down while you're recording it, then rest assured that's how it will sound to the listeners as well. If you're writing or recording a song and it begins to feel forced, then you should probably stop for a moment and pick it up later. It doesn't matter how much formal knowledge you have in songwriting, if the song is not coming from a place of truth, then the listener will recognize it as simply just another nice beat amongst many, but they will not be moved enough to embrace it. Several times, producers have tried to get me to change my sound to fit what's trending or hot at the moment. I never felt comfortable doing that because doing so goes against the grain of everything that has allowed me to experience the success that I enjoy today. Ultimately, if doing what's trending causes me to sacrifice my sound, the lyrical substance of the songs and who I am, I'm not doing it.

Play every game like you've lost all the games before. You only have to win one time to be considered a winner.

—C. RICH

4

THE SCALES OF BALANCE

KNEW THAT GOING after my dreams would have its challenges, but I also knew that failure was not an option. Life does not always give us the things that we feel we need to succeed. We often have to use those missing links and disappointments to create our own links that lead to fulfillment. For instance, not being raised by a father figure has often derailed many dreams and prevented many visions from coming to fruition. Not having that vital component of a male role model in my own life, I tapped into my inner desire to be better. So, for whatever reason, it was never really a big deal for me. It didn't deter my drive to succeed and my relentless pursuit of music as a career. And that's the advice I would give any young man who finds himself struggling with the absence of a father figure. Pull on that desire to succeed and allow nothing or no one to define how your life turns out. I did not have a male mentor, but I loved being around K-Ci and Jo Jo's dad. I was around them a lot and appreciated how much focus their father gave in making them better. So, I learned a lot just watching him. It's OK not to have the know-how, but you must have the drive. When I wanted something, I studied those who were already where I wanted to be. I paid attention. It wasn't up to others to make me successful. My inner desire to succeed made me work much harder and learn to make sacrifices.

Of course, there are often diversions that sidetrack your intended purpose. For a while, I mingled in the street life. I honestly think that I'd done the church thing so much and so well that I was intrigued by a change of pace. The transition from church to street was an easy transition because the streets are always present, ready, willing, and waiting to see what we're all made of. I think it initially began because I wanted more. By more, I mean some of the finer things in life, like the clothes that I saw others wearing or the type of cars they drove—the materialism. I always liked to dress a certain way. I felt like the best way to get more of what I liked, was to dabble in the lifestyle that offered it the quickest. Of course, anything that comes too quickly always comes with a hefty price tag called consequences. I don't glorify that lifestyle by any means. As I grew older and wiser, I realized that it was only by the grace of God that I'm still alive and able to share my story. Almost everyone that I was in the *game* with lost their lives in those same streets we ran in. I honestly think it was my mother's incessant prayers on my behalf that covered and kept me.

There were more than one or two close calls. For instance, I dropped off a friend of mine on the corner one day, and fifteen minutes later, I received a phone call that he'd been murdered right where I'd left him. Life wiped out just like that! Then, of course, there were the run-ins I had with the law on more than one occasion. On one occasion, they knocked on my door looking for someone else. I'd opened the door without checking, thinking it was someone else. I stepped outside to speak with them when they asked if they could search the home. "Nope!" was my response. So, of course, that was just an inconvenience for them, so they called and got a search warrant. Fortunately for me and everyone there, nothing was found. On another occasion, I and a friend of mine had literally just driven away from my apartment when right up the street three police cars—lights on, sirens blaring—went screeching past us. "Hey, I think they're going to the crib!" my passenger responded. They didn't realize that they were driving right past us until one of the officers recognized my vehicle and they all turned around with sirens blasting, giving us just enough time to pull over and regroup. By the time we turned the curve, they pulled us over, searched the car, and again, found nothing. Even still, I'd been one step ahead of being locked up and spending most my young life in prison. Every time I had to throw away something, it left me either owing somebody or having to start over and take a loss. That wasn't meant to be a part of my story. This is why today I still believe in second chances. I understand that people sometimes mess up, but if they are trying to get back on track, then who are we to deny them that opportunity. I found my way back through the music. It was my saving grace. Why live a life looking over your shoulder or gambling with life and death when you can use the gift the right way to bring you the same things you're chasing after.

The advice that I would give any males being raised without a father is to think long and hard when coming to that crossroad about choices. Don't allow disappointments, materialism, or bitterness to deter you from achieving greatness. In other words, don't gamble with life. There are no winners in that game. Once those imbalanced wheels are set in motion, it gets really tricky trying to park a car that's rolling out of control. At some point, you must decide to either seek better or continue living in the shadows of resentment.

Gambling with life on the streets is not worth the price you're paying, weighing life and death decisions daily.

I remember a hot-tempered stage I went through during my high-school days. During one incident, I got into an altercation with a guy over a girl that almost cost me my life. I attended Forest Hills High School and we were rivals with Monroe High School. We drove up to Hardee's one night where I knew some of my Monroe enemies were hanging out, but I didn't care. So, of course, an argument ensued. I was dating one of the more popular girls at their school, so of course, tensions were already high. The argument I had with one of the guys from their high school escalated into a fight and during the fight, I was stabbed in the abdomen. Thankfully the blade was not long enough to cause permanent damage, but still, I was damaged. The doctor reminded me that if the blade had been an inch longer it could have caused permanent damage to my spinal cord and paralyzed me for good.

Not all stories have happy endings. Most endings lay dying in the streets or locked away with destinies ruined. I'm not saying it's always easy. I'm just saying it's doable. You hold the key to unlock your own destiny. When you use it to unlock the door that puts you on the right track, then you lessen the chances of having to go through life kicking down doors that have nothing for you on the other side. Left to our own devices, we often allow our frustrations to set us back instead of moving us forward. My advice is to use that negative energy to propel you to where you want to be in a positive way instead of recklessly gambling with your life to get there. The scales are not always balanced in our favor, but that doesn't mean we can't still win at life. When the weight of the world is pulling you down, you must make a decision. Either balance the scales in your favor or allow the weight to keep you at a state of stagnation. It may take several tries before you get it right, but you have to keep going until it works in your favor. Giving up is never an option, and making bad choices only sets you back to square one. I faced so many failures that at one point I did say "forget it all" and just began partying and wasting away. But in the end, all I did was make it harder for myself to correct those wrongs and try to salvage the things that I almost destroyed in the process.

That's why today I dance to my own beat. I don't compare myself to others or determine my success based on their level of success. I'm comfortable with the man I am. To whom much is given, much is required. I get so much love for using my God-given talent that it's only fair that I give every ounce of me back to my fans through the music or at my shows in the form of love. See me in the dressing room, on the stage, or I might pop up in the middle of the crowd right next to you doing my thing, all in the name of love. I am exactly where I need to be at this moment. I am in a good place, and it has nothing to do with anyone else. I don't allow what others think about me to deter me from doing what I need to do for myself or my career. The older you get, the more value you place on things that you take for granted as a youth. You no longer want to live that reckless lifestyle, especially when you realize that others are depending on you to make it. I've come a long way from that hot-tempered teenager chasing temporal illusions of success and material desires. I'm really intentional about the choices I make. After my shows, I don't hang out in clubs or roam the streets. I take pictures with every one of the fans and retire to my hotel room to rest before my next flight. I understand how blessed I am to still be here enjoying the life that I now have, and I don't do anything to intentionally live haphazardly. When I walk into a room, I want my presence to feel inviting, not threatening. That's what the Calvin Richardson Experience is all about.

When you can walk through a door and not say a word but still change the mood of the room, that's what I want those around me to witness. I constantly thank the Creator for keeping me and those around me safe and prosperous, and I never take my success for granted.

Rarely do I have time to hit the reset button, so I release constantly in the music and through my performances. Those who are gifted in the arts understand that anytime there's a need to get away and you can't go somewhere physically, you can travel through the gift. Family is very important, but I can't make time for family by stopping my music. Anything in life that needs balance and is important to you, you figure out a way to make it work. Sometimes I have to put my phone down and focus, but if the phone rings because a contract needs my immediate attention, I have to take care of that. I'm blessed that the people in my life understand this, especially my family. Even with all our unique differences, we have learned to coexist and embrace those differences as an asset instead of a threat. All my children are different with their own personalities. I understand and appreciate the unique qualities they all have. Being a parent, I have learned a lot more from them than they will ever realize. Watching my youngest son grow, he always amazes me by the things he says and does without any coaxing. It's both funny and amazing watching as his personality develops uniquely. As a parent, I'm as positive as I can be because I understand that I am a model of how they view adulthood. Kids are a blank slate. While developing their own uniqueness, they are also absorbing the habits of those closest to them. My children are my biggest inspiration. They motivate me to keep going, to remain grounded, and to mirror the character that I'd like for them to develop. Train up a child, and even when it seems as if he is veering from those lessons, they are still engrained within the depths of their subconscious to remind them to get back on track. Children pay more attention to the things that we do than the things that we say.

I think that we all pull from some source of motivation. When you live and breathe the gift that God has given you, you never want to use it haphazardly. Consequently, we all have something that we pull on to provoke us when we feel like giving up and throwing in the towel. It's not always the same source of inspiration; nevertheless, we all draw from the depths of our well of motivation.

We have to enjoy the moments that life gives us without pressuring ourselves for more.

—C. RICH

5

IF IT MAKES YOU HAPPY, THAT'S LIVING

HAVING EXPERIENCED MANY losses in the past, I enjoy living life to its fullest. Years ago, I was blessed and fortunate enough to not only meet but have an in-depth conversation with, Frankie Beverly. What he said to me turned out to be one of the single most valuable pieces of advice I've received in my twenty-year musical career: "Just have fun; smile; and keep making good music." I carry that advice with me wherever I go. As simple as it may sound, it's very powerful and pragmatic advice. I think sometimes we can take life so seriously that we forget to actually live. I learned to take nothing for granted. I learned from the University of Life that there's always room for growth, an opportunity to take things to the next level. I glean knowledge from positive and negative critics and keep it moving. I allow nothing to stop the evolution of the Calvin Richardson Experience. Tomorrow is not promised; so, we might as well make the best of the moments that we have today. Each day we awake and start our day, we naturally assume that we are going to make it back home at night. Think of the number of people who had that same thought yesterday, but today they're not here to tell their story. Life is fragile, so why live it angry and agitated all the time?

I always get complimented on my smile, but I didn't smile very much as a kid. As I grew older, however, I learned to value and view life from an entirely different spectrum. I take nothing for granted. Instead, I live my life to its fullest potential. I'm grateful for my upbringing because it taught me the value in little things and how to appreciate intangible things. No matter how high I climb, I still retain my southern soul roots at heart. There's a certain rawness in country folks that reminds them to enjoy the sunshiny days, appreciate the gift of rain, and take time to peer into the stars at night. Perhaps it's their connection to nature that allows them to see beauty in the simplest of things. They believe in family and staying connected to their roots. They treat each other's children and families as their own. I remember growing up always surrounded by my aunts and uncles. I gleaned so much knowledge from this familial tutelage that those lessons remain engrained in my psyche today. I have fond memories of being surrounded by music, jokes, laughter, and lessons from the elders that can only be taught by those who've lived those experiences.

I remember as a kid, I was always close to my mother, and for the most part, I knew that I had her approval by the way she looked at me. Don't get me wrong, if I got out of line, she'd get me with the quickness (which wasn't often). Like my other eight siblings, I too had my moments, but the difference was I usually tried to do what was expected of me because it made mom happy, and I loved to see her smile. To be honest, I was always reluctant to sing when put on the spot during Bible study, or in church, even when people came over to our home, but once I realized that it made mom happy being able to say, "That's my baby," I was quick to sing when called upon. In fact, I looked forward to it. After a while, mom slowed with her praise because my grandma had ramped hers way up. She would always compare me to people whom *I* felt were much better than me at singing. She would consistently, without fail, tell me that I'm better than them. It's crazy how being told something over and over, whether negative or positive, will find a place in your head and stay there! Before I knew it, it was as much a part of my life as breathing. Once you believe something and embrace it, it becomes your truth! I witnessed mom and grandma have words on several occasions because my mom believed that keeping me humble, respectful, and teaching me to always show love over all else, was the best way for me to live my life and be loved. I later came to know that she was absolutely, positively correct in her thoughts and her teaching. Later, I got into the music business, moved to New York and started making records and a name for myself. Every time I'd come home to visit, Mom and I would see grandma, and she would always, without fail, tell me that I needed to come home and leave *whatever* I was doing that was keeping me in New York alone. Now she's gone, but the positivity and life-lessons she drilled into my head are as much a part of my success as any of the lyrics to the songs that I wrote or ever had the pleasure of singing. She was right though. The truth is that some of us are better than others in some areas; otherwise, everyone would be at best average. There would never have been a Michael Jordan, Muhamad Ali, Michael Jackson, Prince, Aretha Franklin, Stevie Wonder, Charlie Wilson, Tupac, Notorious B.I.G., Lebron James, Steph Curry, thus Calvin Richardson. You get the point!

When my grandmother passed away, it was a major blow for me, but the lessons she taught and the love that she shared is incomparable. There's something about a grandmother's love that is inexplicably contagious. Once you catch it, you live with it for a lifetime. Remembering my roots is one of the reasons that later in my career, I decided to take my tour back to the Chitlin' Circuit. I enjoy connecting with those who connect with my real soulful sound. Those who grew up listening to this type of music listen with a type of nostalgia that eases them right into the meat of the message, as I'm singing it to them on the stage. I love seeing how they groove to the sound and become totally engrossed in the music. It's almost as if they are in a church service and the preacher is preaching a message so powerful that it moves them to raise their hands and without provocation bellow out hallelujah! I guess whether I'm singing gospel or soul, the goal remains to touch the heart in a way that sends a deliberate message to the soul. I want my music to be the emotional defibrillator that shocks the broken hearts toward healing and ushers in life's gift of joy and laughter.

When I'm on the stage, I am totally in my zone. All around me is a blur. Using my gift and giving it my absolute all is the ultimate high! Though I feel the energy of the crowd staring at me, I can't see faces or sizes, just shapes and colors. I'm gone . . . in my zone, completely caught up in an outer-body, euphoric type matrix, uttering from the depths of my soul. Love, truth, and honest romance are artistically formulated and articulated over varying drum beats, beautifully-crafted instrumentations with precise harmonic melodic structure, and heartfelt lyrical mastery! If you're younger than thirty, you might not understand it, but if you're thirty and over, you know exactly what I'm talking about. It's symbolic of the day you graduate from having sex to making love. It's a type of artistry that can't be taught. It can only be experienced. As an artist, when you feel it, you just know it, and go with it.

Looking back, I'm thankful for all the lessons that I've been taught, and even for all the bumps encountered along the way that no one even knew were there. In the quiet times, and sometimes even amid the chaos, I whisper a silent prayer thanking my Creator for keeping me and those with me safe as we travel through these experiences together. He never let me take my success for granted. When you love what you do, and what you do loves you, regardless of the bumps, if you keep going, success is imminent. The bumps in the road don't break you. They actually make you. A lot of people try to put their pain on a shelf and act as if it never existed, erase it from their history, shun it, and ignore it. Not me. I find freedom in releasing it through my gift of song. Whether I'm celebrating getting over a painful experience or encouraging someone else that pain "don't" last always, I find comfort in confronting it instead of ignoring it.

People often ask how I knew that I wanted to pursue music as a career. I don't think I knew this at a young age, but I did know that I wanted to sing. I loved grabbing the mic and moving the crowd, no matter how big or small. Even without an audience, I was always singing. It's all I thought about. When I worked a full-time job, after work, I just wanted to sing. I remember I was working a corporate job, and I was doing well with the company. I was making a very good salary. I had purchased my first townhome. I had money saved, and life was pretty good. I was then offered a promotion with the option to manage an entire department, and of course a hefty pay raise. This all sounds good, but not only did I decline the offer, but I also opted to leave the company altogether. I decided to throw all my energy into the music. I began recording music, and that is also when I put together the group Undacova. I wasn't fearful about making such a bold move, because I knew that music is what I really had to do. For me, it was never an option. I suppose if I'd thought about the possible repercussions long enough and pondered all the things that could have gone wrong, then perhaps fear may have crept in, but I didn't even give fear time to become an option. I had no doubt that I wanted to make music a fulltime priority instead of a part-time pursuit. Every step that I've taken to achieve success in doing what I love, required a level of faith. No one ever gave me anything. If I wanted something, I had to go get it! If you want something bad enough, you too must go get it. Don't ever let life trick you into sitting around complaining about all the reasons it's so hard. That's time you could have used to create a better life for yourself by pursuing your dreams.

Don't get me wrong, I didn't always get it right the first time. I made my share of mistakes. I fought like hell to keep my identity and sound. I continue to fight to remain at the top of my game. The only difference is that now I compete with myself by continuing to hone my gift. I don't fight with others about what's best for me or being forced to commit to things that I really don't want to do. My only competition now is staring back at me when I look in the mirror. Life is all about evolution. You can't become so comfortable with where you are that you no longer take time to sharpen your gift. I'm always critiquing my music. I listen to it over and over and figure out how I can make it better. There's always room to take things to another level. That is why I always strive to surround myself with those who complement the C. Rich Experience and can help promote continued growth instead of stifling it. I've been able to build a strong team throughout the years who help remove the burden of having to worry about things that distract me from the music.

You will find that as you grow, building a strong team is essential to future success. A strong team is one that knows the vision, is committed to building your brand, and encompasses loyalty. Honestly, this is not an easy task. I had to go through a few people before eventually being able to enjoy a team that encompasses the essential elements that help reflect The Calvin Richardson Experience, instead of deflecting from it. Loyalty is a very valuable asset to me. If you can't trust the people who are closest to you, then you can't trust that your vision is being fulfilled either. Instead, it will be exploited. Still, I always try to give people the benefit of the doubt. I don't just fire staffers on a whim. In the least, I like to usually have a conversation. I understand that sometimes people just get caught up, distracted, excited by the smoke and mirrors. You have to know when to forgive and when to move on. There are times, however, when I've had to move on because holding on to something that stunts your growth also prevents you from experiencing the fulfillment of the vision and the building of the brand. There's never any animosity. I find it's better to free people to find their own vision, instead of holding them hostage to one that they're not committed to helping to build.

At other times, you may also find that you outgrow those who are around you. If they've reached their pinnacle and can no longer grow with the vision, they need to be freed up to find their own passion. I remember, years ago, when I changed the entire band. I had no idea that it would be their last day. It was just another rehearsal, but I realized that our paths had divided to the point where I was no longer able to get the sound that I needed to take the music to the next level, and priorities seemed dissimilar from the brand. That was the day that I realized that it was time to move on. The seasons had changed. I released everyone during the winter months, last-minute, without having a back-up plan. However, I'd also forgotten that I had an upcoming show scheduled where the contract required a live band. "Oh well," I decided, "I'll just have to contact the promoter and revise the contract to a track instead of the live band." As fate would have it, however, the show was canceled due to a snowstorm that had blanketed the city. This gave me enough time to pull together another band, rehearse, and introduce a whole new sound to The Calvin Richardson Experience. The plan of God is strategic. Sometimes life will force us to make some difficult decisions simply to lead us to where we need to be. You don't always have to have the know-how, but you do need to have the drive, the initiative to learn, to grow, to succeed.

We all have things in life that we wish we could have done differently, but I don't allow myself to live amongst regrets and dwelling on "what-ifs". I take the negative things that happen and turn them into powerful learning experiences. I've found that it takes a lot more energy to live in regrets and hate than it takes to just let go, thrive, and remain positive, even when you are surrounded by hate. All too often, people waste energy focusing on the haters instead of celebrating those who celebrate their accomplishments. I've had many reasons in life to become bitter, but I never found it necessary to do so. I allow it all to disintegrate into the music.

I never sought fame. I just wanted to succeed in doing what I loved to do, which is singing. There's a big difference between fame and success. Anyone can experience fame, but to experience success is liberating. Though I'm thankful for both, without the success in singing, then the fame would be irrelevant. It would be difficult for me to enjoy the fame void of being able to share the gift. The love I have for the fans, the natural high I experience while singing in front of the crowd—ultimately, living the dream doing what I love to do— that is my definition of success. Usually, those who chase fame, instead of focusing on the gift that they've been given, miss it. Figure out what you love to do and use it to propel you to where you'd like to be.

For some people, it would be terrifying and unheard of to leave a successful career in corporate America and step out on faith to focus on their passion. But that is exactly what I did. I'm not suggesting that everyone should do this, but for me, it was a no-brainer. Everyone's definition of success is different. For me, it was not about how much money corporate America was offering me to supervise my own department. Success for me was pursuing what I knew I could not live without . . . the music. My motto for success is, *Don't wait for something you want to happen; work hard to make it happen.* I'm thankful for all the bold moves that paid off, but I also understand that there is more to my story that is still untold, and I look forward to experiencing it.

I always look forward to learning more, pushing myself, challenging myself, and taking things to another level. I hear the critics, but I don't allow things that don't apply to me to prevent me from growing or being who I am. The criticism is not always positive, nor kind, but you take the good with the bad. You can't lash out and give up. Instead, you use it as fuel to help you become a better version of you. If you're not ready for controversy, then you're not ready for success. You can't have one without the other. You don't have to intentionally invite it into your life, because sooner or later it comes knocking. I take it all with a grain of salt. I use it to make me better instead of bitter. It makes me lean into the music not leave it. As an artist or whatever your gift might be, you should have that same mentality. You can't just keep laying your gift on the shelf when life gets too tough. You will have to confront some things, rid yourself of some contaminants around you, and oftentimes regroup, but you do not have to keep laying down the gift. Controversy promotes growth. So, when it comes, don't run from it, confront it. The same thing that knocks you down can be the very thing that motivates you to get back up again.

I don't forget the negative press. I use it as a reminder to keep me focused on the goal. I'm not competing with anyone but myself. You will always be your greatest competition, because no one else can be you, and no one else can maneuver your gift as you can. So, don't get caught up in the hype of trying to keep up with others. Focus on bettering yourself and you win. If I can do what you do, but you can't do what I do, how can we be true competitors?

Perfection is a goal that you will never reach, but you shouldn't allow that to keep you from trying. I never forgot the talent shows that I lost because the losses gave me something to keep fighting for. Sometimes in life, we get what we give, and other times, we give what we get! When you give your all, you can have it all. When you allow yourself to give only what you got, then you wind up living a frustrated mediocre lifestyle focusing more on the failures instead of the mission. Healing begins with letting things go that hold you back, and success starts with a determination to allow nothing to stop you. It's part of the motto on my album, *All or Nothing*. In anything where my talent is concerned, if I can't give my all, I give nothing at all. There is no in-between. What's the point of setting out to meet a goal that you have no intention of meeting?

Giving your all doesn't mean that you still won't experience losses, but it means that you use those losses as stepping stones to help you rise to the top of your game. As with any career, succeeding in the music industry requires patience and perseverance. There is no specific way to achieve that success, you just have to gain a determination to win and not give up. Even when the phone is *not* ringing, you must keep honing your gift, making good music, and putting yourself out there. Today's artists have the world at their fingertips in the form of the worldwide web, especially through social media. Use it to your advantage. But most importantly, stay humble, because in this business you'll encounter and have to deal with some unscrupulous individuals. But always remember, it's not about them!

Artists often dream of two things: being rich and famous. Nothing is wrong with this ambition, but it should never be the primary focus if you plan on maintaining a successful career and longevity in the business. I've always felt that if you take care of the gift, then the gift will take care of you. I've never been in the business for the sole sake of receiving a great payday. Of course, we all want to be able to make a living doing what we love, but if you make money the sole motivation, then it becomes much more frustrating as you attempt to break into the business and you become much more prone to failure. Even today, there are gigs that I've shone up to and performed for free. The question to ask in order to be successful is, "What is my motivation?" If you discover your motive, then your intentions will determine the authenticity in which your gift will be presented to others. People can tell when you are not coming from a place of sincerity and truth. When you place all your focus on the material and tangible aspects, without taking the time to perfect the gift, you shorten the longevity of your career.

The same holds true for those chasing fame. You might get it, but at what cost and how long will it last if it detracts from the authenticity of your gift instead of adding credibility to it? Being in the spotlight can be a blessing and a curse. As much as I love interacting with the fans and mingling in the crowd while entertaining, after the show, I like to retreat to the quiet solace of my hotel room and prepare my mind for what's next. Though I enjoy meeting new people, taking pictures with fans, and so forth, I don't hang out in large crowds because that's just not my thing. After the lights are dimmed, I enjoy the privacy of reflection, rest, and peace in knowing that I gave my all, and now I can allow my body and voice time to recuperate to give the next audience the same level of excellence that the Calvin Richardson Experience strives to present at each unique show. Everyone thinks they want fame until they get it and then realize that they should set boundaries to stay sane and to keep from self-destructing. It's why sometimes I give myself a break from social media when I'm not on the road. I use that time to handle personal and business matters. To check out for a while to give me that time to simply be Calvin—the kid laughing and joking in my Uncle J.B.'s living room with all my cousins and brothers just living unapologetically and innocently loving life. Like those kids, we acted out our 15 minutes of fame and enjoyed the music without receiving anything tangible in return. When you can get to that level of enjoyment, then you are ready to share the gift and reap the benefits that accompany fame.

Look at the life of any successful artist, and you notice a common trend. It was often a long arduous road, but for the most part, they took time to enjoy the journey. Take the Jacksons, for instance. They weren't just handed a magical dose of stardom. They practiced from sun up to sundown honing their gift. Even with the difficulties they faced, they maintained a love for the music. They honed their gift and perfected their performances. The music to them was like breathing and it feels the same with me. With anything I have going on, the music always comes first. Perfecting the gift requires a level of vulnerability that marries the music to the underlying message of the song. There are plenty of musicians and artists, but the thing that sets you apart from the rest is your ability to connect with your own unique fanbase that appreciates you as an artist and creator of your own unique sound.

Failure is an opportunity to start over, reset, and succeed.

—C. RICH

6

THE NOT-SO-SUBTLE SECRET TO SUCCESS

I DON'T BELIEVE THAT there's a secret to success because the word *success* has different meanings, depending on whom you ask. The question that many people really want to know is, "How do I become famous?" or "How do I become rich?" I can advise anyone on using their gifts and talents effectively, but that still does not guarantee stardom or wealth. I always say, "You just gotta put in the work." Unfortunately, there are no shortcuts. I spent years singing as a kid in gospel groups before meeting K-Ci and JoJo and traveling with them on the gospel circuit until their transition to R&B. However, I was not a child-star. It wasn't until I became an adult and continued putting myself out there that I was able to achieve my own personal definition of success. In other words, I simply had to "do-me" and put in the work. You must *put in* if you want to get something out. It simply all boils down to loving what you do and allowing what you do to love you back. When you earnestly use your gift for the love of the craft instead of the lust for potential fame, the gratification expands far beyond a temporal fix. Being able to do what you love, consistently making life better for others, and being happy doing it, to me that's a success! Early on, had I been asked the definition of success, I would have materialized it with the obvious things that most people equate with success: money, cars, clothes, houses, the number of places you can afford to travel to, etc. But I've learned that living in your purpose, being able to maintain yourself, and following your dream is the true definition of success. I don't perform simply for the money. Many times, I've shown up and performed at venues for free, and then there are other gigs that were offering me money that I turned down.

It took me a while to realize my own success because I was chasing something that, to me, was a success at that time: a platinum album, number one record on the radio—which after several albums didn't come. However, I met, and know so many people along the way who'd achieved those things, but later in life had to find other things to do to maintain themselves. I'd see people who'd sold millions of records, but now work behind the desk at a mortgage company, but I was the one buying the house or working as a car salesman, but I was the one buying the cars, etc., I realized success is not about how much you can get; it's about how much you give.

I'd put in years of work before I was able to retire at the age of twenty-one. Retiring doesn't mean I took my spoil of goods and went home to do nothing. It means that I no longer had to work a nine to five job. Instead, I could place all my focus on perfecting the music and building a career doing what I love. Before you can enjoy the wins, you must first learn to appreciate the losses. I took quite a few losses, but I didn't allow the losses to make me quit. Instead, it gave me something to strive for even harder. It's not my success that taught me perseverance, but instead, it was the disappointments I experienced while reaching for success.

Becoming successful is only part of the struggle. What you do with that success after you achieve it is what ultimately determines how long you'll keep it. Attitude plays a major role in how far you go. There are people I've worked with in the past, but I would not care to work with them in the future. It has nothing to do with their talent. Ultimately, it's all about the attitudes, integrity, and negative vibes. Because of the years of blood, sweat, and tears that I've invested in building my brand, I try not to allow anyone or anything around me to taint the creative flow. Long after others have gone, the gift is always there, so you need to make sure you always respect it with the utmost integrity and authenticity. Never take it for granted.

Even when it seemed as if things were going too slow for me, I always attempted to maintain a positive attitude. I knew I had the goods to produce the vision I saw for myself; it just took a while for me to gather all the tools I needed to grow it to a level where I finally felt a sense of accomplishment. I strive to surround myself with positive vibes and creative energy. Intuitively, I always knew that I would sing. However, it can still become frustrating when things don't happen according to your own timetable. I still never allowed that to prevent me from making good music. Even when I went on my hiatus, partying, blowing money, and not taking any gigs, I was still going into the studio and recording. It's a funny thing when you have a gift. You might try to let it go, but the gift is always tapping you on the shoulder to remind you, "Hey, I'm still right here. So, what are our plans for today?" It grabs you by the collar and yanks you from your slumber. The more you ignore that tug, the more miserable you become.

You may have been born with the gift, but it doesn't mean that anyone is going to give you the success you desire to accompany it. I never allowed closed doors to prevent me from singing, performing, or recording. I always found a way to produce good music and share it with the masses. So that's what I mean when I say, "Do you!" Whatever your talent or gift, do it to the best of your ability. When I perform, it doesn't matter how large or small the crowd, I don't hold back—all or nothing!

The fundamental elements consist of putting in the work and treating others with the same respect that you require for your own wellbeing. What you put out, eventually comes back. So, make sure that the things coming back to you are goodness, kindness, loyalty, gratitude. This is not to imply that every bad thing happens due to something negative you put out there, but it's just a reminder that the same way you treat others as you climb, somewhere along that ladder, you *will* run into those people again and need them to help you get to that next level. Although I do not allow anyone to work for me for free, I constantly have people offering to help build the brand or introduce me to new opportunities in the industry. They all say the same thing, "I appreciate you staying true to who you are and continuing to be kind to those who support your music," or "You're just a cool down-to-earth dude," which is code language for you're not the *untouchable* that we often see in the industry. Whatever the lingo, I appreciate the compliments and that I'm able to touch the hearts of so many with the music and the personality. Success entails more than just sales. It's making someone smile, giving others hope, becoming an inspiration to keep going for those who feel like giving up. So, while you're "doing-you," make sure the *"you"* that you're doing is leaving a beautiful legacy.

I'm always critiquing myself. Riding in the car to the next venue, the music is blaring through the speakers drowning outside influences, and voices, I'm deeply entrenched in thought: *"I don't think I'm going to sing that tonight . . . think*

I'll switch it up a bit . . . this song goes so hard, can't wait to sing it live to this crowd . . . I need to make sure there are enough roses for the ladies in the crowd" and so forth. For me, it goes beyond just being successful. I'm actually living my dream, which goes far beyond mere success. It is a blessing, and for that, I am eternally grateful. When you can be paid doing what you love to do, it doesn't feel like the toil of work. Instead, it's the definition of freedom. You want to reach that stride where you no longer feel like you're trying to make it happen, but you just begin walking into what's happening. Though it takes a lot of hard work to get there, once you experience it, it's liberating.

I remember the first time I heard my voice on the radio. I was in New York City with the group Undacova after we had just completed the song titled, "Love Slave" in 1996, which was also later placed on the soundtrack of the movie "New Jersey Drive." We were riding in the car with our then-producer T-Ray returning from the studio listening to the hottest DJ at that time in New York, Funk Master Flex, who was rocking Craig Mack—*"Flava In Ya Ear,"* which was on *fiyah!* Then he blended in our song, and we went CRAZY! For me, it changed everything from that moment moving forward. Hearing my voice playing back to me from the radio spoke to me and touched so deeply. I knew I had found my purpose.

The experience of discovering success is unique for everyone. I have made many friends with artists in the music industry, but realize we all have our own unique stories, and different roads we traveled to discover our own unique definition of success. The common denominator, however, is consistency. I often say, "I gotta give the people what they want." I say this a lot because I believe it. I may feel deeply committed to one of my singles on the album, but if the statistics reveal that the people are having a love affair with a different song, I step back for a moment and allow the union between the listener and lyrics to become as one. That's the Calvin Richardson Experience that I want to maintain—to give the people great music and allow them to enjoy it in a way that never feels forced.

When people ask me to critique them, I always say, I can give advice, but I don't give critiques. I say this because I don't want to become the defining force behind someone potentially changing their sound or who they are. I will, however, share three principles that I incorporate into my own life. These are not the one-two-three steps to success. I don't believe in steps to success because everyone's journey and situation are unique. These are simply some practical principles that I incorporated into my life to keep me motivated as I worked toward my goals and ambitions.

1. MAINTAIN YOUR UNIQUENESS. I never wanted to come across as a person who just wanted to sell records. I always knew I wanted to sing, but I also wanted to share my experiences and move people through song. As a successful artist, you can't achieve this by pretending to be someone else. You don't want to come across as a karaoke copy-cat singer. You want to allow your true self to be introduced to the world through the music. Be honest with yourself about what you want and who you are, because, without that authenticity, the process becomes grueling and tiresome instead of enjoyable. Consequently, you wind up giving up when you should be going all in. I remember butting heads a few times with the industry because they wanted a different sound than I was willing to give. Or they wanted me to sing what's trending in a certain genre, but it just didn't sound like me. I couldn't do it.

2. FOCUS ON THE GOAL. If I had taken time to consider all the obstacles I could have faced early in my career, I doubt if I'd ever taken the plunge to just go for what I wanted. Make wise decisions but don't make excuses. Success does not have anything to do with where you are at this present moment. Look at the countless success stories of people who grew from nothing to overcome insurmountable obstacles. I was a little country boy singing gospel music in little country churches. But that one encounter with K-Ci and Jo Jo's mother changed my course. Even after that encounter, however, I still had to put in the work to earn my definition of success. The point is, keep practicing the gift, *do you,* and the gift will make room for you. The world is your opportunity, but you alone decide where the opportunities take you or leave you stranded.

3. DO WHAT WORKS. I receive advice and suggestions all the time, but if it doesn't work for me, I don't do it. As you learn to do what works for you, you have to let go of the things that don't work, especially the things that hinder the work.

Hard work is not always equivalent to success. You could just be spinning your wheels and not going anywhere. Make sure you're being productive and enhancing the gift and the brand you're trying to build. I work hard taking care of the business side of my singing career behind the scenes. By the time I hit the stage, I've already been on the phone throughout the day working deals, creating the clothing line, approving contracts, the list goes on. The performance that the people see is a result of all the hard work that my team and I have successfully implemented behind the scenes. So even when I am exhausted, I never let the fans see the fatigue, because they came to escape their own tiredness and relax, listen to some good music and have a good time. The fatigue I often feel is not the annoying kind, however, that most people experience while working. Even when I'm tired, I feel fulfilled because I am now living my dream. There were times I was sick on the stage and had spent the entire week trying to recover and get my voice back on track before I hit the stage to perform. On the side, behind the curtain, the team was serving up tea right before I walked onto the stage, grabbed the mic, and performed as if absolutely nothing was going on. If I were working a regular nine-to-five job, I might have called out, but when you are doing what you love, calling out is not an option, but the last resort.

I never took the time to ponder the possibility of failure when I decided to pursue singing full time. That's how passionate I was about making it happen. I could have easily accepted the promotion at my job and lived a nice life. But "nice" was never my goal. My goal remains freedom to allow my gift to work for me in a way that is both gratifying and real. I don't make music for the radio. As long as the fans can connect with the music and I can make it available to them, then I'm cool. When I recorded the song, "Sang No More," that's where I was, at the moment. It wasn't so much that I didn't want to sing, but after I left Hollywood Records, I just didn't want to be part of the industry anymore. I knew I'd still sing, but I just didn't feel like battling the machine of the music industry. My focus since then has remained to stay true to my own unique soulful sound, focus on the creative side, and ultimately, stay connected to those who support the gift by continuing to perfect it. Doing it my way is much more gratifying and beneficial to the brand. I never wanted to fall into that industry trap of commercialism—making music according to what's hot or trending instead of making music that's birthed from the soul, my soulful sound. I plan to sustain my career without selling out to the game of just selling records. Soulful music came from the church, and when it's ingrained in the depths of who and what you are, it doesn't go anywhere. So, trying to act as if you have a different sound comes off as a forced attempt to sound like something that you're really not. The sole purpose is to remain connected to the fans. Once you have a clear vision of where you see yourself, it becomes harder to compromise that vision for the sake of someone else's purpose. I do believe in taking advice, especially from those who have my best interest at heart, but as an artist, you can never allow yourself to become someone you're not. Longevity in your career is more likely if you allow your uniqueness to take over instead of being a copycat of someone else.

Figuring out success is often like trying to manifest in real life the perfect relationship that you see in your mind. You know what you're searching for; you can see, feel it, and even experience it in your heart, but you just haven't physically manifested it yet. So every time someone tries to hook you up with a person and it doesn't quite feel right, you reject the hook-up. It doesn't mean that it's a bad hook-up, it just doesn't feel right for you and you know you won't be able to do right by that person. Ultimately, you navigate the ship that either sails you toward your success or sinks the entire ship. I never allowed the defeatist attitude of others or their expectations to steer my course. There's only one Calvin Richardson. Others may have the same name, but they can't do the same thing. Likewise, I can't do what they do. I'm only interested in doing the best me that I was placed on this earth to do. I don't focus on what I can't do, because the things that I do, I do them well . . . sometimes above and beyond my own expectations. Reach for the stars, and once you reach that goal reach to the stratosphere. I will never stop perfecting who I am. There is always room for improvement. Complacency is a career killer. I always look forward to taking things to the next level. Whether it's the music or the clothing line, paying special attention to the details boosts the image of the entire brand.

When it means something to you, you do what it takes, and give it the attention that it needs to continue reinventing and perfecting it. Simply put, it all boils down to not allowing the fear of failure to dictate your productivity, goals, and aspirations. You hold the power to set your own limitations. Depending on others to give you a stepping stone to success will leave you disappointed and frustrated. There were occasions when I became frustrated because the label was not pushing as hard for me as I knew they should have been, but that's the nature of the industry. I never allowed that to prevent me from doing what I needed to do to gain success in the business. I always knew the gift was larger than the machine that often steers the industry and controls the growth of many talented artists today. If you don't believe in yourself, you will find it nearly impossible to survive when it comes to the business side of the music industry . . . or anything you do in general. My mentality is to never reach my pinnacle because that only means there's no more room to grow, and even when I reach the very top, I'll continue seeking that next level.

Be unstoppable, not because you don't have fears and doubts, but because you refuse to be held back by them.

—C. Rich

7

STARS ARE BORN

E VEN AT A very young age, life gives us a glimpse of our future. If we pay attention, we are constantly dabbling in destiny. Frustration comes, however, when we feel hindered from expressing our core beliefs, seeking our destined path, or when we feel that for whatever reason our gift is being stifled. When you freely express who you are, people are naturally placed in your path when you need them the most. As you remain focused on being happy and living out your own destiny, you attract to yourself what's needed to become successful. No matter where you go in life, those are the people who forever remain engrained in the core of your being. We all have good friends or acquaintances whom, although we don't speak to them daily, we understand that they are always there. Those are the people that you keep embedded in your mind as you're on your quest of doing what inspires you and fulfilling your destiny.

I remember receiving a text message from Mrs. Anita Hailey, whom I affectionately refer to as Mama Hailey. She was congratulating me on my success and how proud of me she was. Her encouraging words meant the world to me because I often reflect on how instrumental she was in setting in motion the wheels that now keep my dream career rolling with ease.

The message between the two of us reads as follows:

Me:

> I tell people often mama that you are the reason that made me believe that I was even good enough to be doing this. When I met you it changed my direction in life I honestly don't where I'd be had you not walked in when you did! You're truly an angel sent from heaven! I'm forever grateful mama. I love you dearly

Mrs. Hailey:

> I will always save this text!! To me there was always something special about you!! I only told two people what I told you that day and that was you and Puffy Shaun Combs, and whenever I see him which isn't often he says he remembers what I told him!! I feel good knowing that God was in it from the beginning ... Don't thank me Baby thank the Lord above! You were destined to be who you are .... 🖤 🖤

The fact that she saw something "special" in me and decided to do something about it, continues to encourage me. She could have simply complimented me and kept going, but her belief in me provoked her to go that extra mile. These are life's unexpected blessings that you should never take for granted. I will always remain grateful for her and her family for embracing me as one of their own and enhancing the confidence that my mother and grandmother constantly instilled within me to be the best *me*. Those who mentored me and were closest to me throughout my life never pushed me to sound like anyone else or to do anything like a copycat of another person. They always reminded me to stay grounded, remember who I am and to be the best version of Calvin Richardson that I could possibly be.

As mentioned, I was raised around women who were very instrumental in helping me to become the person I am today. They were always very honest and upfront individuals who didn't mind telling me the truth—good or bad. Their words originated from a place of honesty and sincerity. It's part of the reason I can somewhat gauge what makes a woman happy and how to tell when she's bothered, even when she is trying to cover up her sadness with a fake smile. I used to love doing things to make my mother smile. I loved it when she was happy. I also noticed the different moods she'd adapt whenever my estranged father would come around, which wasn't often. I'm sure she experienced many disappointments in life, but one of the things I admired about her is that regardless of her mood, she never treated us differently. She was a stern disciplinarian, but also loving and fair. She always stressed the importance of respecting others—to treat others as you'd like to be treated. She, along with my grandmother, drilled that into my psyche, for which I am forever grateful. Their tutelage also taught me to remain humble and get to know others on a deeper level. I learn a lot about a person by noticing their nonverbals, which often speak louder than their actual words.

A person's body language, what makes them laugh, frown, or uncomfortable says a lot about a person's personality. It's like listening to a person say one thing, but you can tell that he or she doesn't agree with their own words. I've always felt that getting to know the person beyond the words helps you to know the true essence of an individual, and it teaches you how to deal with each person as an individual instead of a collective whole. In other words, I allow people to be who they are, and in doing so, it helps me to determine on what level they're placed in my own life—friend, foe, stranger, business acquaintance, inner-circle . . . you get the picture.

I never try to change a person, always keeping in mind that people don't really change that much. They will, however, alter their behavior to suit you while in your presence on occasion, which is not always a good thing. It's one of the reasons people are shocked when someone they've known forever suddenly acts shockingly out of character. If you really think about it, it was always in the person to act that way, but it was certain conditions that brought it out of them and shocked those who thought they knew the real essence of who they were. I've even experienced this in the past with people whom I'd hired. They begin as very nice, humble, and cool people to be around, but the more they traveled it seemed the more "out-of-character" they became. I realize the limelight can be intoxicating to some who haven't experienced it, so I don't hold it against them, but I have had an occasional pep talk to help place things back into proper perspective.

One of my greatest accomplishments is having built a fan base who not only enjoys the music but who also seems to enjoy me as a person. While I do understand that people are fickle as they sing your praises one day and crucify you the next, I'm honored to say that I honestly experience more of the positive vibes than the negative experiences with my fanbase, which is why delivering excellence, a memorable experience, is a major priority. The difference between a great show and a horrible show is the sound. You can have a great audience, but if the sound is not right, then people will say it's a bad show. Such is life. You can be on top of the world one day and the next day become the infamous celebrity that everyone loves to hate. Stay humble always and remain in a state of gratitude, remembering always that you are often only as great as your last feat. I'm not what people expect. I'm not trying to live a celebrity-based life. It's the thing I think that draws people to me or leaves an impression.

People see you on stage and build an opinion, but their real perception of you is sealed once they meet you in person. Having the past teachings of my elders in my ear prevents me from forgetting where I came from or being cocky and rude to those who are just trying to say hello, take a picture, or share a quick story about how one of my songs provoked them to change. If I could advise some of the newer artists coming into the industry today, I would say, "Never become so blinded by the lights that you forget to show kindness to those who help keep you on the stage. Take your time with people; show them love."

It's much easier to just relax and be yourself than trying to show others how great you are. I often see the travesty of those who begin in the business, so kind and caring, but after the climb, they begin to look down on those who helped get them there. It's not that they've turned into another person. That person was always there, lurking, unnoticed. Once they arrived, however, that is when their "true self" began to shine. Money and the limelight are like alcohol. They tend to reveal the true essence of a person. It's disappointing because I can often see how they're hindering their own success.

The fans inspire me to keep striving, to keep creating, to not take life so seriously, but instead just relax, love, and enjoy the ride. By paying attention to the details, I find motivation in some of the unlikeliest places. I'm very observant of my surroundings. Even when people sometimes think I'm distracted, I'm paying attention to just about everything around me: the couple ignoring each other in a restaurant; the vibe of a crowded room; the stillness after a storm; the quiet, yet ageless wisdom of the elders; the newness of love exuding from honeymooners, the list goes on. People, in general, inspire me. I've always been an observer: happy people, upset people, in-love people—I notice and learn from all types. The nonverbals speak much louder than what someone is saying: body language, what makes someone laugh or smile, their unique style of dressing, their taste in music, food, the type of circle they hang with and so forth. I guess we all do this subconsciously, but because of things experienced in my past, coupled with my creative edge, I suppose my tendency to notice things has naturally become like breathing. It's just something I do without provocation. Oftentimes, when life slows down a bit for me, I remember some of the things I've noticed or experienced and these events, memories, and emotions find their way into my lyrics.

No Plan B for Me

While writing this book and reminiscing about all the things that got me to this point, I realize that I absolutely did not have a Plan B. And that is what I mean when I say, "Do you!" Sometimes you have to turn your back to the naysayers and just go for it. I'm glad I never took the time to seriously consider all the negative consequences I could have encountered while fulfilling my dreams. To me, doing what I wanted to do—the music—was a no-brainer, a must. If I didn't do music, there would be no ideal job for me. Anything I'd be doing would make me a miserable employee because I wouldn't be happy doing it. It's the reason I left corporate America after being offered a promotion. Though that sounds risky for most people, I knew what I needed to do, and I went for it. Even growing up as a young teen, I worked a few jobs, but I was never at any of them for long periods of time. Music was my obsession. So, no matter what I was doing, I always managed to somehow incorporate the music into my day.

I'm innovative and learned to do a lot of different things, but I kind of always knew that I would make a living doing something pertaining to using my gift of singing. In high school, I was a bus driver, which paid about $250 per month. It was a convenient way to have money to purchase some of the things that I wanted and drop a few bucks in my mom's hand on occasion. I also remember accepting a job a McDonald's. I was basically looking for extra cash for the summer, something easy I could do inside an air-conditioned facility. When I got to work, however, I realized that I would not be ringing up orders or flipping burgers inside with the comforts of the AC. Instead, the manager led me to a shed outside with lawnmowers and other yard equipment. That's how I found out that I would be working on the grounds! I was *not* happy. It was a scorching hot summer, and I had *not* gotten this job to spend my days frying beneath the relentless southern sun outside. I remember mowing about one strip of grass when my friends drove up. They weren't there to pick me up or anything, just to kick it, grab some food and be gone. But drenched in sweat, when that car pulled off the premises, I made sure I was inside of it. I seized the opportunity to jump into their car and left there as fast as I could. I left the lawnmower sitting there on the lawn and never even returned to pick up a paycheck! I suppose even at that young age, life was revealing the mentality I'd have as it relates to my obsession with one thing: the music. I don't believe in living a life of misery and doing things that I hate to make a living. If you're going to work hard at achieving something, at least let it be something that you don't mind doing, that you're passionate about or love to do.

I tried many different things and didn't mind exploring new obstacles or teaching myself new talents. One thing that my curious mind always enjoyed was being able to figure out how things worked. I loved taking apart things and putting them back together or creating something new. I even took a maintenance class at a technical college. I was always very innovative. Once I took apart a regular fan and used it to make a ceiling fan. I felt like it would be easy. As innovative as I was, however, I never really liked to study in school. My mom knew I wouldn't study, but I did enough to pass the classes. I wasn't very active in sports, but I did play football for a short period of time. I didn't stick with it, however, because it was too hard trying to get to practice. Although there were two cars in the household, when my stepfather would leave for work, he'd take both sets of keys. We lived like an hour from the school in Wingate, so that made it impossible for me to participate in any afterschool activities without a ride. So yes, I experimented with many different talents, as most kids do, but I always knew that it would all eventually come back to the music.

The Early Years

Like most kids who grew up during my era, we were required to play outside. There was no such thing as sitting inside all day playing video games, or anything for that matter—especially with nine kids crammed into a two-bedroom home. North Carolina summers were usually perfect to accommodate those childhood requirements. We'd meet up with the other neighborhood kids outside and kind of just makeup games to play throughout the day: playing in the pond, throwing on boxing gloves and punching each other—basically just living the country life. It's that fearless, creative ingenuity that allows kids to explore life uninhibited. During those early years, our personalities are being developed, experienced, and challenged. It's also the stage that helps determine how we react to life during our adult years. That's one of the reasons I believe in allowing kids to express who they are, to feel free to become the persons they were meant to be. Of course, when I grew up, things were a bit different, and amongst many adults, the belief was that children should be seen, not heard. It wasn't that they were trying to be mean or vindictive. It was simply all about respect. For instance, the saying, "stay out of grown-folks' business," meant that you didn't question the adults about their private matters, and don't dare interrupt their conversations. It was simply the Southern way. While I still embrace many of the teachings, I make sure to incorporate my own new-generation principles when it comes to my own children. I allow them the freedom to express how they feel with a bit more liberality. I teach them about things that we never learned about, such as being a good steward over their finances, maintaining a reputable credit score, and so forth. But I also make sure to teach them the same things my mother and grandmother taught me when it comes to having respect for others. Staying humble and being secure in who you are.

I always cherished my grandmother for constantly reminding me of how gifted I was. She was very instrumental in developing my mentality to believe that I could do anything that I set my mind to accomplish. Her words went a long way. When she'd say things like, "You know you're better than them, don't you?" she didn't mean it in an arrogant way. She was just reminding me that my gift is not something to take lightly and that compared to others I was already exceeding expectation. For a kid to hear that was a major ego booster. So, I do my best to motivate my own children to discover, appreciate, and live their own greatness. My children are my greatest inspiration. I want to always make sure I leave an open door for them to discuss with me whatever topic they choose. To ask questions. To explore their options. And in all things, to remain humble, respectful, and confident. Children are constantly forming opinions and perspectives predicated upon their surroundings and who is pouring knowledge into them. Sometimes the knowledge they receive is detrimental to their growth, especially when it comes from unmotivated under-achievers. That is why they need room to grow and leeway to fulfill their own destiny instead of being forced to live out a destiny that we, as parents, were never able to achieve.

One person I remember who impacted me growing up was my elementary school teacher, Ms. McMillian. She took a lot of time with me, and she'd always show me favor. Then when I went to middle school, Mrs. McAfee was the teacher I remember. Everyone thought she was mean, but I'd always make her laugh. I guess teachers have to somewhat build that wall so that students don't become too familiar and to maintain that control, but with me, she relaxed her guard a little. She saw my drive and that I was going in the right direction and she'd always ask me to stop by. Children will always remember those who impacted their life, the good and bad. This really hit home when I had my own children. I was initially just chasing a dream, the music. Everything came second. I would go see them, but my solid presence wasn't really there. As I grew as an adult and parent, however, I really began trying to get it right, especially since my own father was not present in my life growing up. I never wanted my children to experience that same void in their own lives.

I think you learn more by *doing* and *experiencing* instead of living through the experiences of others. We can take good advice and avoid many pitfalls, but ultimately, we must live out our own experiences to effectively share our uniqueness with the world. I learned a lot by stepping out and doing things on my own. Even in my failures, I gained valuable learning experiences. I'm not advising anyone to live haphazardly, but just reiterating the importance of not always second-guessing yourself. Leave room for failure while preparing for success. In other words, don't be so cautious that you fail to try.

Diligence!

Diligently working to achieve your goals motivates and inspires others to reach for their goals. Diligence is the mother of good fortune and success.

—C. RICH

8

THE ENCORE: NO REGRETS

AS EXPERIENCE GOES, with the knowledge that I've learned, there are definitely some things that I wish I'd done differently in my younger years. I came into the music industry very dependent on the label. Had I not allowed myself to feel at the mercy of the labels, most likely I would have excelled much earlier in my career than later. There were so many things I had to learn on my own, such as not spending the money, but instead investing it back into the business, it's branding, and marketing. My music was even being placed in the wrong sections of the stores. Consumers should know who you are, and they need to be able to support you by purchasing your product and supporting your brand. I realized that many people didn't know who Calvin Richardson was. So, I began watching other artists and learning the business. I learned a lot from those who had been in the business much longer than I had been acquainted with the industry.

Now, however, I'm completely independent, which is much more liberating for me. After realizing that I was stifling my own growth by being so dependent on the industry and longing for them to take my career to the next level, I learned how to take control of my own destiny. Then I started to grow. When I make the statement: "Do You . . . without them," I'm emphasizing the importance of at least trying to reach your goals and visions without always considering what others think. I don't object to wise counsel, but ultimately, when it comes to most things in life, you will have to figure it out on your own, considering what works best for you. I'm grateful that I sought out many of my lifelong dreams at a young age, full of zeal and expectation. You often get out of life what you expect, so set your expectations accordingly. Imagine the audacity of fulfilling a dream! I grew up with many renown artists from North Carolina. It's unfortunate that many of us had to leave the state to achieve our goals, but when you know what you want, you do what it takes to achieve it.

Of course, there were moments when I questioned it all and considered throwing in the towel. But even in that experience, I released the emotions through song. I released "Sang No More," a single from the album released in 2008 called *When Love Comes*. I came into the music business with high expectations early on and was disappointed a few times by the albums falling short of my expectations. I felt like I was paving my own path and veering from the direction that everyone else was going. So, it made my path a little bit longer. Nevertheless, when people express to me how I inspire them through the music, it assures me that I made the right decisions by not giving up when I felt discouraged. One thing I learned is that you don't get what you deserve, you get what you work hard for. You may experience some bumps and bruises, but if you remain committed, keep working, keep persevering and doing something every day to reach that goal, soon you will arrive. I live by the quote that *anything worth having is worth working for.* So, you must self-evaluate and ask yourself, *How bad do I really want it?*

I've learned throughout the years that you cannot be all things to all people. Though I made some mistakes early in my career, the one thing that I'm grateful for is remaining true to who I am and going after my dreams and desires at a young age. I think the older we get, the more cautious we become and the more we begin overthinking things and talking ourselves out of achieving our goals and aspirations. The worst thing you can do is wake up one day and realize that you spent your entire life pleasing others while failing to do what makes you fulfilled. I suppose if I had taken time to consider all the things that could have gone wrong by chasing a dream with such vigor, then I too may have talked myself out of some great opportunities. You can never do enough to please everyone. As you are giving yourself until you give out, people are going on to do what's in their own best interest. Consequently, if you're not careful, you can begin to feel left behind, like you should give up, or let go of the dream. My drive to succeed was never fueled by what others were doing with their lives. And I never allowed myself to remain in my seasons of stagnation. I think when you celebrate the success of others instead of feeling resentful, life naturally begins to yield its goodness to you. What keeps me grounded is the memory of once feeling like I was failing, not succeeding at the pace that I should have been excelling. For instance, there were many songs that I *knew* were going to be a hit, but it just didn't happen like that. So those things really grounded me. Therefore, I'm realistic with all of it: the fans, the marketing, and promotion. Those things are all the game-changers. It dictates where I am and where I could be. I no longer get frustrated when a song or album doesn't perform as well as I thought it should because I've learned that regardless of where the music shows up on the charts, it's still affecting someone.

That's why I respect the new music and new musicians, even if the genre or vibe is not my style. Of course, I will always remain committed to the authentic soulful sound, but as long as an artist remains true to himself, regardless of the genre, I'm all with it. To hear a song authentically about life, love, and loss inspires me to continue to delve beyond the surface and dig into a realm of truth. When I'm in the zone, I create from the depths of the soul to express from a place of unadulterated perception. It's what gives the audience an experience as opposed to a listening session. Just know who you are. Never just take "no" for an answer. Even when it doesn't seem like it, your hard work *will* eventually pay off. You may have to take a step back and figure out what works and what doesn't work, but eventually, you will find your niche and run with it. As you grow, you appreciate the value of enjoying the experience, loving what you do, and taking nothing for granted.

It's not always about winning awards or the pats on the back. It's the meaning behind the praise that counts. Since being nominated for Grammys, I've won several awards. One of my most cherished awards is being inducted into the North Carolina Music Hall of Fame. The North Carolina Music Hall of Fame honors those from North Carolina who have made significant contributions to American music. Their exhibits showcase singers, songwriters, musicians, and producers from various genres of music with roots in North Carolina. Surrounded by family, friends, and loyal fans, I was humbled to receive such a prestigious award after years of fighting to "do me," to maintain the authenticity of the Calvin Richardson sound and making music that has touched the hearts and souls of so many. North Carolina is home, so when I got the call that I was receiving the 2018 award, of course, I was beyond ecstatic. It's something that no one will ever be able to take away.

So, this, in essence, is only part one of the Calvin Richardson story—a southern boy from North Carolina who had enough zeal to turn his big hopes and dreams into a reality. There is no ritual to activating creativity, producing a new sound, or going after what I want. There are no steps that I trigger when deciding to take things to the next level. I don't believe that we should become so stringent in our way of doing things that we leave no room for life's little surprises. I honestly rarely know what the day will hold. Even when I have a set schedule, it's likely to change. Regardless of what I'm doing, however, I try to always take time to enjoy the journey. Oftentimes, we become so focused on getting to the end of the goal and getting the accolades that we miss irretrievable opportunities to notice the beautiful sunsets, bright horizons, and nature's beautiful surprises along the way. Take time to stare out of the window. Peer into the sky. Listen to a conversation without being distracted by your phone. Enjoy the performances as much as the fans. One of the highlights of my show is passing out the roses to the ladies. I love their reaction when they realize that we're at that part of the show. Sometimes they rush the stage. Sometimes, if I don't hold the roses high enough while trying to give them away one by one, they rip them from my hands. Still, it's all in good fun. I enjoy the enthusiasm, and it's just a small gesture of thanking them for their support throughout the years. I love the fans because they always expect a stellar performance, and that's a compliment to how they feel about the music, the artist, and the experience. On stage, I zone in to the energy. It's no longer just me, but it's the C. Rich Experience that the crowd is vibing to, and I love it. I enjoy watching them sing to their favorite tunes. It further energizes my already hyped vibe and anticipation.

After the show is over, the second part begins. I enjoy hanging around for a while, taking pictures with the fans, listening to their stories of how they've been impacted by certain songs. I love it. I embrace it. It's who I am and hope to remain. Everyone wants to leave a legacy.

Hearing my name announced at the 2010 Grammy Awards was a very notable milestone and memorable occasion of my career. The category was Traditional R&B Vocal Performance. I competed with Beyoncé, Anthony Hamilton, Boney James & Quinn, and Ann Nesby. Though Beyoncé won the Grammy, it was yet another opportunity to show gratitude for the blessing of music that kept on giving. In general, however, I simply love what I do; consequently, it continues to love me back. I love everything about performing, from preparing behind the scenes, performing on stage, and mingling with the fans after the shows.

I've been blessed to have several memorable collaborations that remain monumental experiences, such as the collaboration with Babyface on the second album for Hollywood Records in 2004. Though the album was never released, it provided some of the best material I've recorded to date, one of which, Charlie Wilson, formerly of the Gap Band, re-recorded and released as a single in 2005 titled, "There Goes My Baby." That single became a smash hit for him and made us all lots and lots of cash over the years. Even more memorable than that single, however, was the collaboration with Angie Stone. After I had recorded the solo album for Universal Records that I had co-written with Eddie F, Darren Lighty, Cliff Lighty, and Bilal, this album was never released, but similar to "There Goes My Baby," which captured the attention of Charlies Wilson, this album found its way to Angie Stone's attention, who was a very prolific writer in her own right. Angie had a very reputable resume dating back to the late '80s being a stand-out in the rap group Sequence, but she'd gone solo and had a nice radio hit titled "No More Rain," released by Clive Davis of Arista

Records. She was mostly known for the relationship with the talented D'Angelo, co-writing some his biggest hits like Brown Sugar, which catapulted him to be one the hottest stars and sex symbols of the late '90s.

So, when Angie came calling, a lot of great things followed. Not only did she invite me to sing this song with her on her *Mahogany Soul* album that was released in 2003, but she also was gracious enough to take me on tour with her and Maxwell, where she strategically positioned me as one of her background singers. She'd bring me out to perform "*More Than a Woman,*" which became a highlight of her show and ultimately got me a meeting with the godfather of the music game himself, Clive Davis. As fate would have it, an offer followed shortly after for me to join Clive's roster along with, not only Angie but Luther Vandross, Whitney Houston, Alicia Keys, and more. "Yep, all of my failed attempts were sure to be behind me now!" I remember thinking to myself. I had an actual contract with The Don. My lawyer had the contract, and as usual, he was taking his time looking over it; so Angie and I wasted no time getting into the studio in New York City, where we camped out for a couple of weeks recording great song after song with huge hit potential. Our creative chemistry was like few with whom I've ever worked. Angie was truly a borderline genius. Sounds like a story made for a movie, right?

I was living that life, young, rich but not-so-famous. Angie and I were showing up all over NYC at exclusive Arista parties with Clive Davis. We even went to the movies with Luther, just she and I. No one would believe this. I couldn't believe it myself, but it was happening, just like that. Angie was an angel. She even got me on stage for Michael Jackson's, "We are the World 25th Anniversary" to perform with Michael Jackson along with Angie, Beyoncé, Alicia Keys, Mariah Carey, the list goes on. All of this was taking place in short order. We were in the studio working, hitting up the city in

New York, on the A-list flying first class flights to California for the Grammy Awards. I remember being out in Cali in 2004 for the Grammy's; Angie called Raphael Saadiq so we could go to his studio to listen to some of his material to see what was available and what we liked. Raphael was a top producer/writer and hitmaker at the time. We walked in, and he was working on a track for his album. But according to him, he was stuck and couldn't come up with any lyrics for the track, which was a monster! Angie introduced me and told him how dope of a singer and writer she thought I was. He dapped me up and put me right on the spot, asking, "Can you get on the mic and come up with something for this?" Next thing you know, I was in the booth on the mic. He started the track and I started singing off the top of my head: "Hey, excuse me please; you sure look good to me, with your straight hair or braids, kinda got my mama's ways, how about the possibility of you and I, baby. Say you're wit it, if you're not wit it, then excuse me!" He went bananas, and before the night was over, Angie and I were featured on not only that song, but two others that were featured on his album titled "Instant Vintage." During the recording process with Raphael, my attorney called and asked if I was sitting or standing. The irony of the story is that Hollywood Records made me an offer for four times the amount of the offer that Clive had outlined in his offer, and I didn't refuse. That decision changed my life!

My prayer is that my life would remain one of positivity, love, grace, and hope—to treat all as equals. If by chance, any should ever ask, "Who is Calvin Richardson?" I hope that the answer would be one of a positive response: "He is the soulful singer who touches the heart and with one experience leaves an indelible impression that invokes love not hate—the Prince of Soul, the one who inspires listeners to love again." I Am Calvin Richardson.

May all that has been reduced to noise in you become music again because, without a song in your heart, you miss the melody of life.

—C. Rich

THE EVOLUTION OF C. RICH

Courtesy of Kevin "KT" Terrell, 2010

Courtesy of M. Medina, 2010

Courtesy of M. Medina, 2011

Courtesy of M. Medina, 2012

Courtesy of M. Medina, 2014

Courtesy of Kevin "KT" Terrell

Courtesy of Bossidential, 2017

Courtesy of Bossidential, 2018

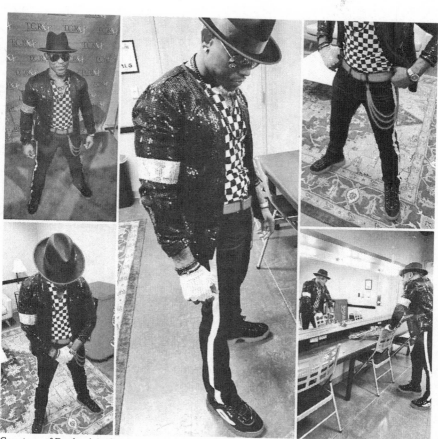

Courtesy of Raphael Anderson, 2019

Courtesy of Raphael Anderson, 2019

Courtesy of Raphael Anderson, 2019

Thank you
for riding with
The Calvin Richardson Experience

Continue to *Do You!*

Courtesy of Raphael Anderson, 2019

DISCOGRAPHY

1. *Country Boy* (1999) – Universal Records
2. *2:35 PM* (2003) – Hollywood Records
3. *When Love Comes* (2008) – Shanachie Records
4. *Facts of Life: The Soul Of Bobby Womack* (2009) – Shanachie Records
5. *America's Most Wanted* (2010) – Shanachie Records
6. *I Am Calvin* (2014) – BMG
7. *All or Nothing* (2017) – Shanachie Records
8. *Gold Dust* (2019) – Shanachie Records

ABOUT THE AUTHOR

AFFECTIONATELY DUBBED "The Soul Prince," Multi-Grammy Award-nominated singer/songwriter Calvin Richardson has been delighting fans with his straight-shooting, no holds barred, southern Soul for close to two decades. *USA Today* declares Richardson is "influenced by vintage R&B and his gritty vocals set him apart from his smoother contemporaries . . . fresh vibes from a singer who respects and values his roots."

Calvin Richardson has written songs for many artists, including Charlie Wilson, Angie Stone, and Raphael Saadiq. Calvin Richardson came by his soulful style honestly. Born in McBee, South Carolina, he grew up in Monroe, North Carolina, the fifth of nine children. Calvin had a strong musical upbringing. His mother sang in the local gospel group, Wondering Souls. He and his brothers sang in their own gospel group called The Willing Wonders. He was, however, able to listen to secular soul music. He was particularly inspired by Bobby Womack, Sam Cooke, Otis Redding and Donny Hathaway. Singing on the gospel circuit, he met and became friends with Cedric "K-Ci" Hailey and Joel "Jo Jo" Hailey, who went on to form the hit-making group Jodeci in the early nineties. Calvin was inspired by their success to form the urban contemporary vocal group

Undacova, whose song "Love Slave" was included in the New Jersey Drive soundtrack in 1995. When Undacova folded, Calvin launched a solo career that resulted in his debut solo album *Country Boy* on Uptown/Universal Records in 1999. The album included a great cover of Bobby Womack's "I Wish He Didn't Trust Me So Much." While Calvin was working on this follow-up, Angie Stone heard a demo of his song "More Than a Woman" and invited him to duet with her on a version of the song for her album *Mahogany Soul*. In 2003, Calvin's album *2:35 PM*, named after the time one of his children was born, was released by Hollywood Records. The year 2008 saw the release of Calvin's Shanachie Entertainment/Numo Records album *When Love Comes*, with its single "Sang No More" hitting the Urban AC charts. In 2009, success continued via Charlie Wilson's hit rendition of Calvin's co-write with Babyface, "There Goes My Baby." The same year, Richardson paid homage to one of his greatest influences with Facts of Life, his powerful live-in-the-studio tribute to Bobby Womack that garnered two Grammy nominations, one of which was for his duet with Sounds of Blackness powerhouse Ann Nesby. In 2010 he released the album *America's Most Wanted*, and *I Am Calvin* followed in 2014. With the release of the *All or Nothing* in 2017, it is clear that pure soul music is alive and well and the Soul Prince is carrying it forward to where it needs to be. In 2018, Richardson was inducted into the North Carolina Music Hall of Fame. Finally, in 2019 Richardson released the album, *Gold Dust*, continuing the trend of touching the soul of his fans, baring it all through lyrical interpretations of the heart.

Made in the
USA
Lexington, KY